SEMI TRUE

SEASONS ON THE ROAD WITH A PRAIRIE HOME COMPANION'S RESIDENT WRITER AND TRUCK DRIVER

RUSS RINGSAK

The Globe Pequot Press

GUILFORD, CONNECTICUT

Text design: Bill Brown

Library of Congress Cataloging-in-Publication Data
Ringsak, Russ.
  Semi True: seasons on the road with a prairie home
companion's resident writer and truck driver/Russ
Ringsak.—1st ed.
    p. cm.
  ISBN 0-7627-3094-3
1. Prairie home companion (Radio program) I. Title.
  PN1991.77.P73R56 2004
  791.44'72—dc22
                                    2004052355

Manufactured in the United States of America
First Edition/First Printing

CONTENTS

Preface iv

1 Amateur Night at Ray's Truck Stop 1

2 New York by Way of Atlanta 12

3 Suffering an Easy Winter 31

4 A Muscovy Duck and a Flatland Cafe 41

5 The Stunt Baby and the Runaway 61

6 The Loneliest Road in America 85

7 Tomatoes, Love Letters, and Turkeys 99

8 Crazy Horse and Millennium Fever 116

9 A Bookkeeper's Battle with Fiction 131

10 The Secret Champ 141

11 Fightin' Words 159

12 Attitude 178

13 Geronimo and Robert W. Service 188

14 Two Shots 205

15 Cross Country 222

About the Author 235

PREFACE

The following stories and observations were gathered both on the ground and from the seat of a semi, first as an independent owner-operator and later while driving for a Minnesota traveling radio show. For no particular reason I chose to track three touring seasons around the recent turn of the century, from the fall of '98 to the spring of '01, and it's not every place we went during that time and it's not strictly in order. Most of it is true for sure and some is hearsay but from good sources. There is possible outright fabrication in here as well, but I wouldn't be able to pick it out from the rest.

A few segments have been taken from articles I wrote for the prairiehome.org Web site. I included them not so much out of laxity, but because no matter how I tried to keep them out, they seemed to belong in here. They are used with the gracious permission of *A Prairie Home Companion.*

1

AMATEUR NIGHT AT RAY'S TRUCK STOP

EARLY IN SEPTEMBER 1977 I ESCAPED AN office career by selling my entire portfolio, four thousand dollars' worth of John Deere stock, and laying it all down on a new powder-blue R-model Mack costing thirty-eight grand; I also bought six lengths of heavy chain with hooks and six bright red heavy-duty lever-action come-alongs, to tighten those chains; got a bunch of wood blocking, rented a weary but usable flatbed semitrailer, and took it to an empty factory parking lot on a Sunday and practiced backing up for a few hours. The next day I went into a downtown office building and signed on as an owner-operator with an outfit that hauled steel around Minneapolis and St. Paul. There were four other trucks, local guys who had been at it for years, and they were a big help, not out of enthusiasm for my epiphany but out of simple decency. Perhaps even mercy. They all had CB radios and I didn't— it would be months before I woke up and bought one— and I was likely the object of a good deal of radio humor.

Short of warfare, the trucking business probably affords a person with as much opportunity to blunder in full view as any trade known to man or woman. An incident stands out from the early years: It was in the first winter, 4:30 A.M. at Ray's Truck Stop east of St. Paul near the St. Croix River. I had a load of steel pipe bound for the other side of the Wisconsin scalehouse and was unsure of the weight, and Ray's had a scale. Pulled onto the platform and stopped, and they gave me the go-ahead over a speaker to pull off and come inside and get the scale ticket. In my amateur condition I somehow forgot I had a trailer back there, turned too sharp, and ripped a large yellow bollard, a ten-inch-diameter steel pipe filled with concrete, right out of the ground with the trailer wheels. The Mack barely felt it, but I heard a wild squealing back there.

I backed off, parked, went inside, and paid the scale fee. The ticket said I was legal and I told these two tired pump jockeys, looking old before their time and smelling of dirt and petroleum, that I had taken down their bollard. That yellow post out there. I showed my insurance card. I was the only customer. The place was run down, the counter grease-stained to black, two bare sixty-watt bulbs hanging over it. Fan belts from the 1950s hung high along the dirty walls and old wood shelves of parts leaned unsteadily in the shadows.

The guys looked at me blankly, faces dark with grit lines, showing white only around the eyes, staring like a couple of uncomprehending fuel-soaked owls. As if they'd been in some ecological disaster. I said Here's my name and this is the insurance company and here's the phone number, and they just looked at me like I had newly landed from Mars. Neither spoke for a long time. It was a silence where incredulity and disbelief hung in the air, until finally the gaunt unshaven long-haired tall one said: "I didn't see nothin' . . . Did you?"

Without taking his gaze from me, the eyes-close-together thin-mustache heavy one said, "I didn't see nothin'."

And then I realized that it was my own self who was the uncomprehending one, and who was the object of the disbelief. Real truckers don't think like that. They don't initiate paperwork and they don't take blame. A real trucker, if he said anything at all, would tell them they should get that effing post out of the way of a working man. They were accustomed to that; what I did made them think I might be a con man or a cop or some new kind of fool. But I sure was no truck driver.

Even so, I kept at it. We hauled steel to local fabricators, foreign coils from barges in the Mississippi River, and American coils and flat steel from the huge grimy mills down at Gary, Indiana. Smoke and heat, relentless noise, traveling cranes moving overhead, all fire and smoke and commotion in those gigantic old sheds.

There was another notable event that first year. Four of us were at a barge dock in St. Paul where a track ran along the top of a concrete wall on the edge of the Mississippi River. A heavy railroad crane would lift coils from the barge and swing them around to the flatbed parked along the other side of the track. The big hook from the crane went through the loops of a cable harness, which went through the hole in the coil. We would adjust our six-by-six cradles to receive the fat roll as it was being lowered onto the trailer.

The hook was held by a shear pin, designed to be the weakest piece in the assembly, and another driver there was getting the first load, a single coil of about twenty-four tons. Just as it hovered those last few inches over the cradle, the pin broke and the steel whomped down onto the trailer, sending the driver jumping back and causing the rig to bounce heavily and throw up a rush of dust and dirt. This sudden drama made all of us miss seeing the main event behind us, which was the crane falling backwards into the barge.

But we definitely heard it, probably the loudest crash heard in St. Paul since their last train wreck. With the boom sitting crossways to the track, the sudden release of the load had caused the counterweight at the rear of the cab to throw it backwards. It was amazing it didn't go right through the bottom of the barge, and it was further amazing that the operator suffered only a broken arm. The trucker was shaken but unscathed. We figured the crane might have gone through the floor and sunk the barge but that layer of steel coils in the bottom absorbed the blow. The underside of any vehicle is an ugly thing, and it seems the bigger and heavier, the uglier. The underbelly of a railroad crane is a sobering sight.

They call 'em semis because the trailer has no front wheels. It can't roll on its own like a hay wagon but has to sit on the back of a truck, which makes it a semitrailer. The truck isn't strictly a truck either because it doesn't carry cargo, so it's a tractor. The whole rig is a tractor-semitrailer, shortened to tractor-trailer, shortened to semi. Our present tour director insists they are the Front Part and the Back Part, firstly because she is an East Coast city girl and secondly just to yank my chain.

Tractors, and trucks, come in two shapes, cabovers and conventionals. The cabover is the short one with the flat front and the cab that tilts forward so you can get at the engine. The conventional has the big snoot out there that opens without disturbing the rest of the beast, and why they chose such a dumb name for such a sensible design I have no idea. They could have called it an obvious. Or a logical. ("Bought me a new Peterbilt logical two years ago and I'll tellya, it's not the worst dang truck I ever drove . . .") The long-wheelbase ones with the big double sleepers are affectionately called Largecars.

Highway cabovers were born of an alliance of brightly burning safety zealots and dim-bulb reformist politicians—still to this day our most dangerous threat to good sense—who felt deeply compelled to limit the overall length of the highway unit, an oversight that meant the shorter the tractor, the bigger the payload. For many years nearly every freight-hauling fleet in the country ran cabovers—stubby, twitchy, rough riding—until a group of bright folks built the ultimate tractor, a prototype that fit entirely underneath the front of the trailer. Looked like an oversized flat cast-iron ten-wheel Indy racer with the driver extended forward. Had this goofy tractor been produced a trailer could have been eight feet longer yet, with the driver lurking low out there under the nose. It was so ludicrous the dimwits in charge gave in to the lobbyists and did the obvious: They limited the length of the trailer to fifty-three feet, regardless of the power unit.

And what a boon. Nearly all the independents and most of the fleets have switched and cabovers have gone from common to scarce. Conventionals are easier to drive, less likely to jackknife, and far easier to live in. And you can check the engine-room vitals without dumping all your stuff into the windshield.

In retaliation—and not wanting to appear they had for once given in to good sense and the rule of reason—Congress, the do-gooders, and the Department of Transportation then unleashed their collective genius upon the drivers' log books. Oh boy. Instead of the old eight hours of off duty, drivers are now bound to stop ten hours after their daily driving hours are up, meaning those who sleep seven hours must certify that in the morning they hang around the rest area or at a truck stop for three hours before they start driving again. Rules like this provide training for fiction writers. Semi fiction writers, at least.

Barge traffic stopped when the river froze and three of us got laid off. I rented a box trailer and hauled potatoes from North Dakota to Michigan, Ohio, and Pennsylvania, and grabbed whatever I could trip-lease back—generally glass, paper, farm chemicals, or auto parts. Sometimes it took two or three days to find a load. The Mack was a city cab—didn't have a sleeper—and when I'd sleep with my face in a rolled-up jacket on the steering wheel I'd wake up with a stiff neck and a jacket wet with drool. I tried to sleep on a piece of plywood across the seats but there was a problem with the gearshift lever. I usually ended up folded on the floor. When the thaw came we all showed up again in the sunshine of the main dock and hauled steel until late July, when the company told us they were bankrupt. I went through the fall hauling gravel and in the winter went back to interstate potatoes.

I was sorry to leave that flatbed because no trailer is more fun. You cannot personally lift anything that is hauled on one, so it takes you into interesting places with cranes. Pulling a flatbed and still being local was the best of trucking possibilities.

The next summer it was back to the gravel and the following winter I went full-bore into hauling bulk potatoes. Bought a pair of Kenworth highway tractors and two box vans and was lucky enough to hire two good drivers. We'd run two trucks with three drivers, turning two rounds a week, carrying hard reds from the Red River Valley through Michigan's Upper Peninsula and over the Mackinac Bridge to factories out east. Get there early in the morning and eat hot potato chips right off the line while they unloaded us with Bobcats, tearing the hell out of the plywood inside the trailers. A couple of places had the big tilt lift where we'd open the back doors and they'd stand the rig up at a forty-five-degree angle. It looked like a big Scud, ready for launch into the next county. This all worked fine for a while, until the recession came and the backhauls dried up.

I had met Garrison Keillor on a softball team in the early 1970s, when he was hosting a morning record show on KSJN Public Radio in St. Paul. The major sponsor of that show was Jack's Auto Repair, a fictional enterprise with a real softball team; I responded when the call went out for players and ended up the pitcher. We kept in touch and about 1981 the morning record show had become *A Prairie Home Companion*, a live Saturday late-afternoon show with a national audience. I suggested they could save shipping charges if they hired me to rent a truck when they went touring. By then I was easing free of the trucking business anyway, having been weeded out by deregulation and high fuel costs and my own shortage of shrewdness.

They agreed to take me on as a tour contractor. We didn't need a semi and could get by with a heavy-duty diesel straight truck in those early days. I'd reserve one ahead of time, hopefully one with a lift gate at the back, and I learned to inspect these rental trucks real careful to make sure the stinkin' lift actually went up and down and that the air brakes worked, and that the paperwork did indeed cover the states we would cross. If the radio worked that was a bonus. Our gear was heavy enough to put a two-axle truck over the weight limit but most scales gave you a thousand-pound grace factor. We never got more than seven hundred pounds overweight.

The real hassle with running straight trucks wasn't stuff like that but just the fact that they're designed for city work. Taking them cross-country was like running a goat in a horse race. They'd bust a gut straining up a mountain at twenty-five miles an hour. They'd be howling for relief from trying to run full-out all day long. I had a tough lobbying job to get us into a grown-up truck because union rules required a bigger crew and the truck rent was higher. And we really didn't need the extra room, if we packed it tight.

But one spring afternoon a high-pressure fuel line broke in California and gushed diesel fuel all over the apron at a Penske lot near Berkeley. The location couldn't have been better, right there at the shop, but we had to wonder if next time it would be out in the desert somewhere. And that November the engine in a brand-new truck completely destroyed itself on a rainy night in the Allegheny Mountains in Pennsylvania. They had to tow a replacement up from Pittsburgh. It took all night before it showed up at the old truck stop where I'd been towed, and it turned out to be one of the absolute worst unjunked trucks in America at that moment. The rain was still coming down when we parked it back to back and the wrecker driver helped me unstack all five tons of gear from the dead truck and stack it into the one he'd towed up, which was near death itself. It had a gasoline engine and feeble electric brakes, bald tires, a collapsed driver's seat, a small gas tank, a lousy heater, loose mirrors, and no power to speak of, plus it poured smoke out of both the breather and the exhaust. It was the kind of truck refugees use to flee Third World countries during a takeover.

The trip home was a nervous one, making less than two hundred miles to the tankful, but it led to change. The next season we were renting a big rig and it didn't take the tech crew long to appreciate it. All the weighty gear we'd been piling up suddenly sprouted wheels, and loading didn't become fun but it quit feeling like the tryouts for the world's-strongest-man contest. And now, with forty-eight feet instead of twenty-four, we could carry more gear. At any rate, this part-time moving contractor business ultimately led to another new career in 1990, when I was given steady employment as a researcher and driver. For some time I had been passing along road notes and local information that might be useful to our show, and now I'd weaseled my way into a writing job.

2
NEW YORK BY WAY OF ATLANTA

BY OCTOBER 1998 I HAD BEEN DRIVING for the radio show for eight years, and it had been clear from the start that I had fallen into one of the primo assignments in the history of the truck. The tour brought us to a different venue every Saturday, most of them within a two- or three-day drive of the last one. The cast and crew always flew so I was able to set my own route and pace, and since I was also doing research I could stay at motels when the need arose to be at a phone. I never had to find a back-haul, and I knew how every steel-reinforced case and cabinet would fit together in the pack. At about ten tons—the weight doubled after we moved into a semi—the load was not so light as to let the wind blow the truck off the road but it wasn't heavy enough to be a struggle at every upgrade. And when the show was in St. Paul I didn't have to drive at all. I wasn't getting rich and I wasn't driving the truck of my dreams—the Kenworth W900 with a 550 Cat engine and a thirteen-speed transmission—but I had independence and was seeing the entire country. And I had my summers free.

We had a good Indian summer in 1998, but in November the countryside took on the look of bracing for winter. The chill and the overcast meant the agreeable weather was stepping aside, yielding to the reality of bitter days ahead. Time to put away the feelings of being lucky and blessed and all that business and think big boots, scarves, snow throwers, mittens, a good shovel, warm underwear, headgear, jumper cables, a towrope, and maybe even a set of all-weather tires. At the very least a good windshield scraper.

Our show generally made a late-fall stand in Manhattan, and that year they scheduled a stop in Atlanta on the way out. On a Tuesday morning, November 17, at the truck rental yard in the St. Paul suburb of Roseville, I climbed the familiar ladder up over the left fuel tank and sat there at tree house height in the air seat, started the engine, soaked up the heavy valve clatter as it warmed up. A Klaxon blatted on until the compressor brought the air up to the ninety pounds of pressure needed to unlock the brakes, and in the meantime I filled the blanks in the logbook: truck number, trailer number, date, company, address, co-driver (N/A), starting location. I signed the vehicle inspection form, which read like a doleful poem:

I detect
no defect or deficiency
in this motor vehicle as would be likely to affect
the safety of its operation or result in its
mechanical breakdown.

What it really says is *Whatever goes wrong it's all my own dang fault so go ahead and hang me.* The next generation of regulations will likely require the driver to certify a daily self-examination: *I detect no defect or deficiency in my personal makeup as would be likely to affect the stability of my behavior or result in my emotional breakdown.*

When the buzzer stopped I circled the yard to where our trailer was parked, eased back to slide the fifth wheel with its V slot under the nose and into a heavy *clunk*, like railroad cars coupling. When it's exactly centered the trailer doesn't move sideways at all in the meeting; a game to play against yourself, trailer solitaire. The locking bar in the slot grabbed the trailer pin and I got out and made sure of it, cranked up the legs, coupled the air hose gladhands, and plugged in the electrical socket. Checked the lights and undercarriage and she was good to go.

We keep the same trailer but rent a different tractor for each trip; this one was a new Freightliner Century Class with fuel tanks for three hundred gallons, an engine brake for mountain work, air-conditioning, CB antennas, air seats, and a walk-in double-bunk sleeper cab. Bigger than some jail cells and a lot more interesting, but without indoor plumbing. A dash full of gauges and levers and switches, and a computer that read out total mileage, fuel consumption, outside temperature, trip miles, leg miles, gallons of fuel burned, and odd little maintenance notes, like "Recirculating air engaged. Stale air in 20 minutes."

I left the yard and made my way to eastbound I-94. As I approached the bridge to Wisconsin, a voice on the CB said: "Hey Westbound. Eastbound chickencoop open?"

A driver on the other side responded: "Yessir. They be runnin' ya through, jist checkin' yer ground pressure. Didn't see no DOT." If the eastbound driver wasn't sure about how the weight was spread on his axles he still had time to take exit 4 to the truck stop scale and do something about it, like slide the trailer wheels forward or back or move the fifth wheel, where the trailer rests. Without the DOT there he probably didn't have to concern himself with the logbook or if all his lights worked. He at least found out he'd have to be in the slow lane when he got up there to mile 8. Some drivers need to know this stuff and some just like to find out if their radio's working. That old "Breaker breaker one nine, got a copy?" is all long gone, and these days a good buddy is a gay guy.

Around Eau Claire the end of a conversation on the westbound side came into range: ". . . and my brother, he finally gave up on the farm and took a job as a garbage man, but they don't call it that no more. They call him a waste management engineer."

"Yeah, I know, they do that nowadays. He don't sit at a drafting board or a computer, does he?"

"Nossir. Jist goes out in a big ol' truck with a bucket on it and throws garbage bags in there. Hydraulic ram packs it down and he hauls it off to the landfill. Pays a lot more'n farming and he says the hours are better too."

"Copy on the better hours . . . Yeah, cousin on my wife's side, he works at the schoolhouse, big ol' place, and he's a night janitor there but on the payroll he's a sanitary engineer. He claims he never even learned the multiplyin' tables—says if he's an engineer then his dang ol' billy goat is a brain surgeon."

"I swear, they's people who figger you should never use one short word if you can use three long ones instead. They think that shows how smart you are. Like at my kid's school, they call the library the Instructional Materials Center. It does wear a man out, listenin' to that malarkey."

"Four on the malarkey." (Short for *10–4*, meaning "I understand.")

"But anyways, I'm jist glad a truck driver's still a truck driver."

"Copy that. What'll they call us when they find out we still got a simple name like 'at? Transportation engineers?"

"Well, see, now—that'd hafta include bus drivers and

taxi drivers—pilots, too, right? So they'd hafta come up with somethin' about freight . . . somethin' like a freight motion specialist or . . . somethin' like 'at."

"Lord, don't even mention it. Makes my brain hurt, thinkin' about it."

"Yessir, four on the brain hurtin' . . . Looks like I'm comin' here to my get-off, driver. We'll catch you on the rewind."

"Copy. You have a safe one."

"Yessir. Same back atcha."

The CB doesn't have a lot of range, a few miles, and if you're going to carry on much of a conversation you have to both be going the same direction.

You stay cooped up in a truck for days at a time and you can get real conversational when you get the chance. Two hours out I stopped for coffee at a small truck stop on I–94 in the middle of Wisconsin, the Big Steer. Three drivers in the next booth started telling car stories. A guy in a Dale Earnhardt cap said, "My wife's family, they're a bunch of scam artists, the whole gang. And her brother, this doofus named Bennie—Benjamin—you've met him, John, they call him Bones—he's the worst. Last year in that big winter we had, he's got snow piled up along both sides of his driveway about five feet high, higher than his car, and he cuts these notches on each side, where he can see the road, and he sits there, nose in, with the engine runnin', lookin' over his shoulder for a car that looks like somebody with good insurance.

"The road's all slick, hardpack snow and ice, but he's got sand on the driveway for traction, and here comes a new Buick and he throws it in reverse and comes bombin' outa there backwards and the guy hits the brakes and slides and *ka-pow*, y'know, big friggin' crash. So Bones, he jumps out and right away starts hollerin' at this poor sucker about drivin' too fast on ice and what would have happened if it was his kid on a sled instead of his car comin' out of the driveway, whaddya think about that, he's sayin', My kid could be dead right now—and Bones, y'know, he ain't got kids anyway—I mean, he's lucky if he has a date once a year.

"But he's yellin' like he's gonna call the cops, and he wants the guy's insurance company and all this. And he's in the guy's face for smashin' up the rear fender on his beautiful Dodge there, and it's nothin' but a junker—I mean that car is a sorry wreck already—and he acts like he's all mad and stuff. And the guy says he's sorry, like he didn't know it was that slippery, and then old Bones, he turns on the charm and says maybe he shouldn't have got so mad and maybe they should settle this peacefully, without the cops. For maybe like five hundred dollars. And the guy says *'Five hundred dollars? For THAT?'* and Bones says, 'Well how about three hundred,' and they end up at one fifty. Cash money—Bones rides to the ATM machine with the guy.

"He pulled this three times in one day last winter, and again the next day, and then he had to junk the Dodge, but he was gonna do that anyway. He's tellin' me the trick is that you start talking first, and you keep talking, you don't let up until he admits it's his fault. *Then* you act like the good guy. He was thinkin' he was the smartest guy in the whole state, braggin' about it. My wife, she's all embarrassed."

They laughed and John, a bearded man in a camo jacket, said a part-time driver he worked with sometimes did things like that. Last October the radiator core was leaking in the guy's '91 Chev so he went looking for a roadkill deer, not exactly a rare item around there in the fall. He found a fairly fresh one, lifted the carcass into the trunk, and then went to someplace out in the country where he hunts.

He hung it up, just off the ground, tied to a good-sized tree near the road, and then drove into it about twenty-five miles an hour, fast enough to cause a thousand dollars' worth of damage and leave a lot of deer fur in the grille for the insurance adjuster. Got the check and junked the car.

They all chuckled.

"Sheez."

The first man said, "Man. I'm not sure I'd wanna do somethin' like that. That's a little weird."

"What a guy, huh?"

The third man was a wiry guy with a jacket that said ANGEL'S BAIT AND LAUNCH SERVICE. He had a wheezy voice. "Yeah, there's a lot of what I call devious people out there. My wife's hairdresser was tellin' her about how the transmission in her old Toyota was leakin' all over the driveway and it wouldn't shift so she has her boyfriend follow her across the river to Winona over there, and they park it behind a bar and then they come back to a bar in La Crosse and they knock back a few, and they come out and guess what, her car's not there, and they call the cops. So when they find it two weeks later in Winona she's cryin' to the insurance guy the tranny's all messed up and it was running perfect before. And they cut her a check.

"And she's got her own theory on scamming, too. She tells my wife there's two things—first, you gotta stay under two grand, so it's not worth it for them to send out their dogs. And the other thing is timing. You gotta be able to get the timing right. Like you might be thinking about a little garage fire—so you wait for a thunderstorm with a lot of lightning, so the company is gettin' other claims comin' in at the same time, see, so they don't come out to your place and start snoopin' around." The waitress cleared the plates and filled cups; she had brought the check with the meal, like they do in truck stops.

The Dale-Earnhardt-cap guy said, "Y'know, these people, why don't they just work? I mean, if you put that much energy into a job, y'know, you might end up makin' some real money."

The Angel's-jacket guy said, "I think they get a rush from doin' stuff that ain't legal. They like the scam part and they like braggin' about it."

Another driver, a delivery guy in a white shirt, came in during the story and they made room for him. He said, "Yeah. They could get rich. Like me." He was smiling, looked like he enjoys delivering local freight. And why not. He gets to drive a truck and he gets to go home at night. He ordered coffee and pumpkin pie with ice cream and said, "Remember before computers, when you could get rid of a car with just a screwdriver? Take the plates off and they'd never trace it?"

"Oh yeah," said John, "my dad must have junked five cars that way. They'd never take the time to track 'em down."

"Yeah," said the new guy, "I sorta hung out with this bunch of low-grade criminals for a while after I got out of high school, I think they were from Green Bay or someplace over there by the lake. They weren't out to hurt anybody, but they just got drunk a lot and wrecked stuff. So one Saturday we're sittin' in the bar somewhere all afternoon watchin' a football bowl game, I think it was, and the roads are slick and we're in this big old Mercury this guy had and we come out of there and we're goin' over to Stevens Point, I can't remember why, and we go around a curve outside of some small town and he's goin' way too fast and we go straight off the curve and down this embankment and drive straight into this house. Right through the wall. The front wheels of the car are *in* the living room."

"Oh boy."

"And nobody's hurt?"

"Nobody's got a scratch. It's like bringing a pontoon boat in a little too fast, is all. And we get out and knock on the door and there's nobody in the house. They're all gone. So this guy Ace that owns the car, he's drivin', and he's got a screwdriver in the glove box and he takes the back license plate off, and then we go in the house, the door's unlocked, we just walk in the place, and he moves a chair and takes the front plate off, right in their living room. Pictures on the wall and everything. And then we just take the plates and we're outa there. 'Screw the car,' Ace says, 'I never liked it anyways.' We don't take a thing in the house and we walk into town and find a bar and somebody calls their girlfriend to come get us. And Ace, he never hears a word about it."

"You'd think someone would have seen it, or heard it."

"I know. I was wantin' to get out of there real fast. But nothin' ever happened."

John shook his head. "If that was *my* house, man, I would be goin' around askin' some questions. I would want to be takin' down names."

"Ah, they prob'ly just called the insurance. Prob'ly got a whole new paint job and everything."

Next day the countryside through Kentucky and Tennessee was likable, as it is any time of year; the big bridges and wide waterways, the moody green mountains. It's dramatic and it's fun to drive, and it makes you think truck driving is not always the living purgatory it's made out to be, especially by some of its practitioners. And as I was thinking these thoughts about serenity and beauty and about Chattanooga being one of the most sweetly situated cities in the nation, I–59 came up from Birmingham and joined I–24 and shortly thereafter I–75 came down from Knoxville and I-24 ended in a torrent of traffic heading for Atlanta.

The pace picked up through Georgia and at some point it became three lanes in both directions and darkness fell and I was in some kind of Atlanta Hundred-Mile Diesel Sprints, trucks on both sides, passing the one on the right and losing ground to the one on the left. I was bombing along with the hammer down and there was a solid string of trucks ahead and behind, looked like a massive rescue convoy coming to save the city. I was glad I wasn't in a car in the middle of all those big wheels.

Our show was playing the fabulous Fox Theatre, at the corner of Peachtree and Ponce de Leon, six blocks south of Peachtree Street and Peachtree Place. I parked the truck in a rental lot and caught a cab to our most excellent hotel across from the Fox.

Next morning I took the Gray Line trolley ride, which is really a bus, and our guide said there are forty-four streets in Atlanta named Peachtree, which I later verified on the map, not because I didn't believe him but because I wanted to behold this amazing fact in person.

The only other riders on the bus were a married couple from Ontario. Our driver was a pleasant black man, said he liked Canadians: "A big bunch of 'em come down here every year from Winnipeg, first thing they say, 'Take me to the liquor store,' and I do."

He had an impressive knowledge of Atlanta history. It started as Marthaville, a railroad town where train crews changed, slept, took their meals, waited to leave for some other town somewhere down the line. In 1840 the name was changed and it began to grow. By 1860 there were stores, bars, churches and neighborhoods, he said, and then Sherman came and burned it all to the ground. "Now that church over there"—he pointed—"he didn't burn that. He didn't burn any of the churches, because, you know, he didn't want to get on the bad side—thought it might come back on him. But he burned everything else. I heard he burned Atlanta 'cause he heard about the prison camp at Andersonville where the Union prisoners were bein' mistreated, starved to death and all that business. So he burned it to the ground, and he burned everything else all the way from here to Savannah. But he never did burn Savannah.

"Ten years ago Atlanta had a population of nine hundred thousand and now it's three and a half million. All in ten years, and it's still growin'. They tear down stuff around here so fast you wouldn't believe; the historical society in Washington, D.C., got on their case about it, and finally they had to come down here and open an office right here in the city so they could keep an eye on these people tearin' everything down. It's been bad. Tear down everything just to put up new, everything gotta be new here. We got malls everywhere around here, right here downtown in Underground and everywhere out around the city. I guess we're about malled out by now."

We drove into the heart of downtown. "That building right there, that belongs to Georgia State. That's a big university, forty-five thousand, and they own the Olympic

Village now, too. When the Olympics was over they gave the dormitories to Georgia State . . . Now, you see that big gray buildin' over there? That's a bank, the SunTrust Bank, and in that building over there is where they keep the secret formula for Coca-Cola." We drove by Margaret Mitchell Park and he said, "Margaret Mitchell and her husband were going to a play or the restaurant or something, they were crossing the street, and she turned back to get something she forgot and she was hit by a cab and killed. She was forty-nine years old.

"Now here's the Ritz-Carlton. Atlanta is the only city in the U.S. to have *two* Ritz-Carltons . . . Now that building over there—the one that looks like it's got handles on the sides, that's a building you don't ever want to have to go to, because that's the IRS building. Now this here is the Crawford Long Hospital, named after the first man to use anesthesia. Now that was a big step forward when he started doin' that.

"And over there, you see that big building they're working on, that's the Biltmore Hotel. It's empty now but at one time that hotel was known as the Queen of the South. They gonna make offices or apartments there, but they'll have a little bit of the hotel, too, and the lobby and all that stuff." He said that since the Olympics were here everybody wants to come and live downtown. "They got warehouse studios everywhere; people can't fill 'em up fast enough." He pointed out a coffeehouse. "Now that's another thing. Since the Olympics left we got coffeehouses. Never had that before. Now they everywhere."

We passed a small park, now heading north toward the Fox Theatre, and he told us there was actually only one real peach tree on the entire length of Peachtree Street. He pointed out some small trees lining the edge of the park and said, "Now those trees there, they planted 'em here a while back, I think there's about twenty of 'em, but they are not real peach trees. They're sterile. Those are token peach trees; they planted 'em so folks could get an idea what a peach tree looks like, but they don't have any peaches on 'em, and they never will have."

We drove on and our guide said: "After the Civil War it was tough in the South because everybody was broke, nobody had any money, couldn't build anything, so after a while they started up the policy of W-S-B and that means Welcome South Brother. And so then northerners would come down and invest money and they helped to get things started again."

We crossed a bridge at the site of the Battle of Peachtree Creek, scene of some of the heaviest action in Atlanta. Few cities in this country have seen the kind of fighting that went on here, but they've been rebuilding for a hundred years and seem to have put that war into the background. The driver became somber. "A lot of blood on the ground around here. A lot of blood."

We went up to the Buckhead neighborhood, "the Palm Beach of Georgia." He said they called it Buckhead because back when it was all just woods a lot of men would go up there to hunt and right away somebody built a tavern at the edge of the woods. A hunter dragged a deer in there one day and they cut the head off and hung it on the wall and they named the tavern after it, and from that they started to call the whole area up there Buckhead, even after they started building all the fine homes there. Some people wanted to change the name to something a little nicer but it had been called Buckhead for so long they just left it that way. A name's a name, he said.

It was a terrific tour. I recommend it, especially if you're lucky enough to get the driver we got.

I left Atlanta right after we loaded up Saturday night, November the 21st, and headed up Interstate 85, up I–77, on to I–81 and I–80, across the George Washington Bridge and into the big city Monday morning. We didn't load into the theater until Friday morning, so I stashed the truck and caught a plane to Minnesota to enjoy an unseasonably warm three-day break.

Flew back again to New York on Thursday. The plane landed at JFK in the morning rain, not a fancy airport but simple and direct, the signs leading you to Ground Transport, and before I knew it I was in the lobby and the black Lincoln Town Car was sitting outside at the curb exactly as they said it would be. It went so smooth I felt like a mobster on my way to a hit. The driver was conversational and told me the car had 350,000 miles on it, which is remarkable but not unusual. We sailed easily into the city, the massive fantasy of buildings standing before us shrouded in mist across the river, like stalagmites in a foggy cave, and we slipped underneath the East River and emerged right in the center of it all, like swimming under-water and coming up, unexpectedly, in the middle of town.

Forty-fourth Street was blocked because of the Thanks-giving Day parade so I got out at Sixth Avenue. The side-walks were full of colorful umbrellas, bobbing like the start of a hot-air balloon race, and I walked west in the light rain. The sidewalks were covered with wet yellow leaves from the library park across the street; there was a drum and bugle corps somewhere close. It was like Home-coming Day back home: a damp breeze, fall in the air but not real cold, band playing, wet leaves. I had the feeling my high school football team might soon take the field against Park River, our permanent rivals.

I don't get all tingly with excitement over the prospect of going to New York anymore, but the place always has a little surprise for a visitor. I found a good Caribbean buffet near the hotel for $9.50. Three measly dollars more than the average truck stop buffet, but a quantum leap more interesting. Later I ran into our crew and a couple of New York stagehands at Jimmy's Corner on 44th, which has become our East Coast hangout. A hand-lettered sign in the window said, SIGN UP NOW FOR NEW YEARS EVE. Again, it was like walking down the street in my little rural hometown. Well, sort of like that. Vaguely like that, except the owner of my hometown bar wasn't in Ali's corner in the Rumble in the Jungle, when he beat George Foreman in Zaire. Lots of photographs there in Jimmy's Corner, and Jimmy himself is usually there as well.

Friday I got up early and caught a taxi outside the hotel to take me to where the truck was parked on Eleventh Avenue. Drove it to the Town Hall and a crew of trained professionals unloaded it, closed the doors, locked the padlock, and waved me off. I drove uneventfully back to Minnesota for the holidays.

3
SUFFERING AN EASY WINTER

YEAR'S END BROUGHT A FINISH TO THE New York stand, meaning I had to deadhead out there to bring back the gear. I hitched up a sister to the other Freightliner with our trailer and had an easy afternoon through Wisconsin, right up to the stuffed traffic leading into Chicago. Rowed through that and finally shook free and headed east on the I–80 toll road, and when the legal hours were gone stopped at what the tollway euphemistically calls an oasis. I slept in the camel, there on the asphalt with all the other camels. Over the years the Indiana and Ohio turnpikes have become more familiar and less interesting than my own driveway and I've found various small strategies to keep out of trouble, because they not only make you pay to drive there but they also have unrealistically low speed limits, lower on trucks than on the general onflowing surge of humankind. Three good CDs can get me across Indiana but I generally need help from channel 19 on the CB radio to traverse Ohio, although it was fairly quiet at six o'clock that Wednesday morning.

The mountains of Pennsylvania on Interstate 80 are beautiful and the road is fast and there are deer in abundance to keep us alert. Dozens that day came to a bedraggled finish on the shoulder. Out in the woods others quietly found themselves positioned in rifle sights and became venison on the tables of our fellow carnivores, a somehow more natural and orderly passing but a nuance of perhaps little concern to the average buck. Either way he meets a sudden finish and ends up in deer heaven, eating someone's roses.

From scenic Pennsylvania it was up and over the deep-cut Delaware Water Gap, and coasting down into New Jersey was pleasant for a while, at least to the rim of the vast halo of industry around New York City. At some unmarked point I crossed the event horizon and became part of the slogging traffic that causes a certain percentage of the nation's drivers to flatly refuse to take a load of anything into the Big Apple. The interstate started to feel three feet deep in molasses and I wondered if perhaps a mad scientist somewhere had managed to slow down time. Crawled up to the booths at the George Washington Bridge and paid the mighty twenty dollar toll. (It's thirty bucks now.) This was the opposite of a black hole, where everything accelerates as it approaches the epicenter. This was more like a neon hole, into which everything moves slower and slower as it approaches the point of singularity, Times Square.

Saturday night after the show ended I brought the rig to the front of Town Hall; I stood across the street to admire the purposeful long-distance look it had, sitting out of place in that high-walled narrow street at night, tucked against the long marquee, its yellow highway lights all lit up. I walked to the corner deli for road snacks while younger guys dealt with rolling the castered heavy cases up the ramp. About ninety minutes later they waved me off and I idled slowly away, feeling ponderous alongside the sleek limos, a grouper among eels in the tight shallows of 43rd Street. Hooked a wide right at Tenth Avenue, picked up speed on the big one-way and headed north to catch Broadway at Columbus Circle, and at 10:30 P.M. I crossed the George Washington Bridge. There's no toll, westbound; it's your GET OUT OF TOWN FREE card.

I cleared the event horizon and made it across Jersey, slept in a Pennsylvania truck stop lot, and slipped into Ohio Sunday noon. The eastern part was an easy cruise for a good part of the day. CB reports kept coming in about the abundance of police protection up the road, but I was locked on a Werner truck fifty yards ahead and holding it at about sixty-seven miles an hour. The truck limit is fifty-five there, one of the last vestiges of Jimmy Carter's legacy—for cars it's sixty-five—and they've made a real industry out of enforcing it. This guy seemed to know what he was doing because every time he slowed down we met a trooper, either coming the other way or sitting in the middle.

A hundred miles from the Indiana line I started to chicken out a little. We passed a couple of semis and I was no longer optimistic about sailing twelve miles per hour over the limit into infested territory. When I cleared the front truck I let the Werner guy go, backed down to fifty-nine, and moved into the right lane. And just as I did that an eastbound cop came at us, braking hard and swinging a quick U into a gap in the concrete median barrier, a gap you don't see until you're right on it—then pulling tight alongside my running board. I could see into his car, the radios and the computer pad and the other cop gear there. I figured he may have nailed me when I was passing but it was more likely the Werner truck up ahead. He took off and a mile up turned on the disco lights.

They are a sneaky bunch, giving to erupting into sudden U-turns and zapping the first misbehaving truck coming at them ("takin' his picture") and then whipping another U-turn to run him down from behind. They work hard for the state, out there on the road conducting stickups on working men and women, and now that the eastern part has fewer miles of median they seem to double the dose in the other half. With fifty-three miles to the border I came to an underpass where there were three of them working the same spot. One had an eastbound truck, one a westbound truck, and one sat in the middle waiting for me. In that western hundred miles I counted twelve patrol cars.

The amateurs in the cars and pickups are pretty much left alone; they get nailed once in a while but they have that extra ten miles an hour to play with, so it's the pros who are the real prey. Knowing the cops monitor channel 19, truckers openly refer to Ohio as The Communist State, as in, "Well here we are back in The Communist, so git your wallets out."

I cleared Chicago and found a motel in Wisconsin, and Monday morning there were thousands, possibly gazillions, of ducks in the sky over the central part of the state, from the 108 mile marker to the 88 on Interstate 90; twenty solid miles of waterfowl wheeling overhead, a fabulous sight, like the entire sky in motion. Except I thought, What the heck are you hanging around for, you silly birds; this is December. Don't you have any idea what this can all become? Or do you guys know something we don't?

Pulled into the truck yard around three that afternoon. The pickup was waiting on the gravel outside the chain-link fence, dusty and dirty, a beautiful sight. It was overcast and blustery, a real bite in the air, and it seemed that finally the warm-weather party was winding down and by late night there was frost on windshields and winter could not be far off. But then Tuesday it dawned clear and warm and at 9:00 A.M. water was dripping off the metal roof of the barn, bright sparkles gathered at the edge and catching the sunlight as they fell into the brown spears of dormant flowers. It was springtime again.

It felt ominous. Another winter like the last, I figured, and we might well be overrun by hordes of southern Californians, coming north to the good life, building overblown condos and turning old elevators into toney restaurants with bags of seed lying around. Bringing New Age and Cowboy Chic, fouling us with their New Country and New Age music and their impossibly optimistic narcissism. They'll think we're cute. They'll think fishing is cute. They might find wild turkeys cute, too, and elaborate wattles could become fashion statements. And they'll see deer hunting as an abomination against Bambi and they'll hold awareness groups against it and silent protests at the capitol.

They would be moving onto status farms and raise registered show Holsteins, slim cattle with delicate small udders, bred for aesthetics and grace rather than milk: Arabian Holsteins, Minnesota Walking Holsteins, Fox Trotting Holsteins, Standard Bred Holsteins, Hackney

Holsteins, Saddle Bred Holsteins. In upscale restaurants we'll hear things like "They're raising *lactose* cows? Oh, how yucky! I mean, like, *Hello?* Like, where are these people *coming* from? I mean, *she* looks like a cow and her *cow* looks like a cow."

In my personal Minnesota paranoia, feed mills were about to become theme gardens and total mind and body spas. Silos would be converted to vertical tubular energy-channeling axial vortex-unifying convergence centers.

We needed a punishing ripping slashing raw bleak freezing stabbing fifty-below Siberian-whiteout death-dealing truck-tipping car-burying train-stopping airport-closing power-outing ruthless killing blizzard here and we needed it soon. It was December. It was supposed to be Minnesota but out on the road Harleys thumped by and Sunday we saw a frog cross that same road. A *frog*! It wasn't supposed to be the season of frogs and Harleys. The earth needed to travel 292 million miles to the other side of the sun for frogs and Harleys. It was sixty-six degrees out on Tuesday, just short of seventy here on Sunday, and sixty-eight again on Wednesday. Men were hanging Christmas lights on their houses in shorts and tank tops. People were golfing. Snowshoe hares were hiding out because they turn white not when the temperature changes or the snow falls but rather when the days shorten in length. They knew how they stood out in the woods and were keeping concealed and quiet. Coyotes and foxes were on the move. There were verified mosquito sightings. Bats were flying; they normally hibernate in September and October. Winter birds were staying north, the snowy owls, redpolls, and pine grosbeaks. Bad signs, and we hoped it was temporary.

Because nothing keeps Californians away like a blinding blizzard on national TV: trucks stranded, roofs of cars barely showing in the whiteness, power poles down, farmhouses covered right up to the eaves, cattle frozen stiff. Hooves sticking out of snowbanks. People leaning nearly horizontal into a white blur, one hand cupped around the mouth and the other stuck out straight ahead, groping blindly. Hefty snowplows, barely visible, throwing high drifts up into the whipping punishing winds. Scenes from cafes, shell-shocked ordinary citizens mumbling, "I dunno, I was just drivin' along and she started to snow and I never thought nothin' of it and pretty soon it was really comin' down and the wind was whippin' and the next thing I know it's two feet deep already and I can't see nothin' and I'm slidin' in the ditch and the whole world is white. I was lucky to get help; I guess it just wasn't my time to go. The big guy upstairs was lookin' out for me I guess . . ."

All across the country people see these images and say: "Those people are idiots to live up there. We would never live there." We northerners needed this. We were coming to the place where a lot of us were getting nervous, even those indoor wimps like myself who had been grinning happily through all the months of warm weather.

That Wednesday morning the sunrise lit the whole sky softly ablaze, with a pale blush along the edges. It got warmer as the day went on, a day where more and more people became more and more uneasy. Waitresses said, "Yeah, it's great but we're gonna pay for it later so may as well enjoy it while we can." Hard for a working person to enjoy it, of course, because by 5:00 P.M. it was dark outside.

Crocus and daffodil bulbs, planted for the winter's duration and intended to delight in April and May, were sadly opening; fooled into thinking winter is over, like a patient waking up from the anesthetic before being wheeled into surgery. A woman told me her strawberry plants had white blossoms. Possibly a fatal case of optimism on the part of that plant.

Another woman said she was puzzled and apprehensive of the weather, so misty and so warm, and wished she could enjoy it more, but when you break an old record high for December 1st by a whopping eleven degrees— sixty-eight as opposed to fifty-seven—it just makes a person nervous. I agreed. We seemed to be having warm June days with a total eclipse of the sun at 4:35 every afternoon, day after day. She said she also disliked the way everybody was always saying we were going to pay for this later. "Hell," she said, "we're always paying, for every-thing.

"But," she added, "it does have that feeling you get just before the tornado hits."

4

A MUSCOVY DUCK AND A FLATLAND CAFE

AND THEN JANUARY '99 CAME IN AS A real below-zero January, at last, and our show was in town for a while so we could really wallow in it. Walked in shirtsleeves out to the mailbox on Monday morning in the minus-thirty-five windchill and thought how similar it was to swimming underwater: I knew I could not last long in that medium. I must change that which surrounded me or I would die in the next few minutes. It was an exhilarating experience, but when I got back into the warm kitchen I tossed the paper on the table and kept a straight face as if nothing had happened. As if I hadn't just stared death right in its icy eye.

When it gets bitterly cold like that in Minnesota, past the stage where you can throw on a jean jacket and take the pickup on some errand—say, run to the store for juice and a dozen eggs—it also gets more crowded. You know it's actually *less* crowded because of all the people who have pulled up and smoked on out of here, but because we wear these big puff parkas and the caps and gloves and all, we need more space around us.

In cold like that three or four people are all it takes to overcrowd an average convenience store. They can't pass in the aisles. They have to step back to let someone in or out of a doorway. And the harshness of the cold makes the other's errand seem unnecessary and stupid. I think, Why would that idiot go out on a day like today for corn chips and cheese dip? You'd think they'd have more sense than that—risk their stupid life for some dumb nachos.

We're all bigger and slower and less patient than when the cold is manageable, up there in the twenty-above-zero range. Down under the zero mark, especially after a few days, we get bulky and cranky and it doesn't take that many of us to make a crowd. (We didn't know it on that fourth of January, but it would be five years before we got another below-zero daytime temperature reading in the Twin Cities.)

The Minnesota Vikings' bright promise of greatness and a for-sure trip to the Super Bowl were squashed Sunday, the seventeenth of January, 1999, in the NFC Championship Game on a missed field goal, missed by a man who hadn't missed a single one in almost two years and who might be the greatest field-goal kicker in the game. We still had a one-touchdown lead but on the miss we caught that familiar whiff of catastrophic failure in the offing and we were right, our Vikings were undone, and the silent winter suffering began in earnest. And it wasn't really suffering as much as the resumption of our natural condition. The euphoria of having our team with sixteen victories and only one defeat, our team poised to finally win the Super Bowl, which we surely would have won if we had made it there because how could we not, after losing it four times already—that big-time euphoria was so unnatural here we hardly dared speak of it.

It felt good but a lot of us didn't trust it, and with that unthinkable missed kick in that awful fourth quarter there came the familiar giant sucking sound of optimism being vacuumed out of the state. The Goddess of Doom herself drove our boys backwards down the field, yielding up the tying touchdown in the last minute, and then Doom's twin sister Disaster fell on them in overtime. In the last three drives our once mighty team was tossed around like a bunch of pathetic old rag dolls with stuffing coming out.

It's always that way when the game gets big enough for folks to get together with friends and have some snacks and chili and a refreshing beverage; I've been to at least ten of those gatherings over the years and don't recall the Vikings ever winning a single time. Not once. When everybody makes a big deal about it and has parties and big get-togethers, they get grim and we're done for.

We never made it. We fell short. This great and powerful team undone by inevitable fate, as we always are. It has always been a team in touch with its fans and, more specifically, the fears of its fans. We expect the worst and our Vikes are right there with us. Maybe the problem is in the name; the real Vikings were brave and ruthless but somehow just never had it in them to rule the world. And nearly everybody else in Europe and Asia did, one time or another: Greeks, British, Spaniards, the Macedonians, the Mongols, the Egyptians, even the Italians. Even the French. But the old Vikings just raised a lot of hell and then faded without ever really getting the whole enchilada.

Should they have been named the Minnesota Mongols? The Minnesota Macedonians? It has a rhythm to it. But the problem's not in the name. They could be who they are under any name. At any rate, once again the season for the Purple ended with all of us walking around hunched over, wearing our heavy clothes and slushproof boots and holding a sour taste in our mouths. Even though we sought comfort in the fact that we had the most exciting governor on the planet at the time, underneath it was still the same miserable old winter doldrums for Minnesotans. The Christmas lights were still up on the main drag, including the center one with the big wreath and the letters that say NOEL coming into town and LEON when you leave, but the cheery welcome was fooling no one. It was January. Summer was half an orbit away, over there on the other side of the sun.

But speaking of Jesse Ventura, there was one small consolation, even in losing to a warm-weather team like Atlanta. Our governor bet their governor a case of lutefisk against a case of peaches on the outcome. Either way, we would win that bet: Either we'd get a case of delicious fresh peaches or we'd get rid of a case of bad-smelling eight-month-old codfish soaked in lye.

We got over it. The football. It's our seasonal humiliation and it'll happen again so no use to worry about it. And it's not as bad as it could have been, because humiliation increases with how late in the season it occurs—losing the Super Bowl is worse than losing the conference championship that leads to the Bowl. Not making the playoffs isn't as bad as losing in the first round. It's backwards. It's the Theory of the Inverse Letdown—the closer you get to the prize the more excruciating the pain. Or the better the team, the more catastrophic the collapse.

Our show was in town for a stand at the time and I drove up north to see our farm friends Paula and Emil. She told a story about a one-footed Muscovy duck named Matilda. The meat of Muscovy ducks is generally darker and leaner than your average duck meat, and whether a corollary can be drawn or not I don't know but along with leaner meat you get a duck that is not as bright as the average duck. Paula said she thinks ducks are generally as smart as pigs and that you can get a lot closer to a duck than you can to most animals. Older people used to insist that the Muscovy duck is actually part turkey but duck breeders say this is simply not true; no truth to it at all. They may act like turkeys sometimes but you don't have to have dumb relatives to act stupid yourself. Still, Paula said, nothing looks dumber than a duck perched on a roof peak.

Most ducks, after drinking in cold weather, will go sit on straw or some other dry bedding and tuck their feet up under them to keep them warm until they dry, but a Muscovy will often go sit on a perch somewhere and act like it's summer, like it couldn't care less. And this is what Matilda did, and froze her left foot so badly it turned dead black and they had to bandage it. Paula would put half an inch of lard in a sardine can and set it on back of the stove, on the ledge next to the chimney, where it would get just warm enough to melt, and every three hours she'd get up and put that warm lard, mixed with a little sulfa from the pig house, on a rag and take it out to Tildie. "She'd come thumping right over to me," she said. "She knew that warm lard would feel good. After a while the foot just fell off and I kept treating the leg until it healed."

When the bandage came off for good all she had was a nub down there; it looked like the bottom of a drumstick. Which it was. She walked funny, even for a duck, but she got around the farm pretty well and seemed not too much the worse for the experience. She could walk a straight line but couldn't swim one, and she left an odd set of footprints. Other than that, she hadn't changed all that much.

Early that spring a neighbor, Tom Rullifson, stopped in to borrow a couple of saw horses. He sat and watched Matilda for a while and said, "How much you want for that duck?"

"That duck isn't good for much; she wouldn't be any good for setting on eggs, for one thing."

"No, I know that, but I might find some use for her."

"What are you gonna do with her?"

"Well, we'll see; if it works I'll tell you about it. And if it doesn't I might just have roast duck. That's all you're gonna do with her, aren't you?"

"Well, eventually, yes."

"So do you want to sell her?"

"I might. I'd think about it."

"What would you have to have for her?"

"Oh, I'd probably take four dollars."

"Four dollars . . . huh."

"What did you want to pay for her?"

"I was thinking about two."

"Well, two, I don't know if I could take two. I mean, I know she's only got one foot, but two is right down there. I guess I'd think about three."

"Well, I'd give you three, maybe. That's about as far as I could go."

"Okay then, three dollars. You tell me how she works out."

Matilda had a brother named Francis Drake whom they called Franny. There was a big White Leghorn rooster on the place named Freddy Fairbanks; the Muscovy duck is also known for being feisty and Franny and Freddy would square off in the yard about every other day and fight it out, duck to chicken. They'd circle each other, feathers puffed out, looking fierce. They didn't bite. They'd leap at each other, go at it with their feet, trying to knock the other down, wings flapping, creating a hell of a ruckus.

In their last fight they were having at it at the top of the stairs to the root cellar and Franny got the upper hand, so to speak, and knocked Freddy backwards and down into the stairwell, the Muscovy following on top of him. There was a very loud *thump* when they hit an empty wooden crate at the bottom. Paula's skinny father-in-law Lawrence was sitting daydreaming in the yard under some trees and that loud *thump* startled him and he jumped up and said,

"Jesus Christ and God O Mighty!"

When they got to the rooster Fairbanks he was dead, either from the fall or from an overload of excitement. A rooster and a drake, bitter longtime enemies, fighting it out to the finish, like in the movies. They didn't dress him out but just buried him, thinking that the meat would be bad if he died that way, all stressed out like that. I wondered about that, thinking about chickens I had seen running around farmyards with their heads cut clean off, but it's true those chickens probably had no idea they were in deep trouble, right up until it all went black. Fairbanks saw it coming.

Anyway, when Tom Rullifson brought the saw horses back Paula asked how Matilda was doing and he said she was working out just fine. "So how did you put her to work?"

"Well, when I was here last time I noticed in spite of the bum leg she walked real straight and she had about the right stride so I used her to plant beans. I tilled my garden and set corn at the end of the row and she'd walk right to it. I'd just go along behind and put a few beans in each hole."

Paula said, "It was a sad day for me when Tom Rullifson died. He was truly a madman. I laugh every time I think about him."

• • •

I didn't see a groundhog on that second of February, a Tuesday, but there was an opossum out under the spruce trees, moving unsteadily on the snow crust, occasionally breaking through. He was looking up into the branches, sniffing the air. All creatures have their own beauty of course, but possum beauty is an elusive attribute that an unsophisticated person like myself cannot appreciate. He did have a shadow, and even the possum's shadow looks undignified. A cardinal flew in and landed on the ground below the nearby bird feeder, as if to show him what lookin' good looks like.

Had he been a groundhog—what we midwesterners call a woodchuck—we would be in for six more weeks of winter, but we're in for that anyway as a matter of course. But Groundhog Day's a good holiday, neither religious nor commercial, connected only to the planet's flight plan, now halfway between the winter solstice and the spring equinox.

The shadow part of it is shaky science, but they have a passable record over there at Gobbler's Knob in Pennsylvania where they conduct the ceremony with old Punxsutawney Phil, correct about 59 percent of the time since 1980. A person might be able to make a nervous existence betting on sports with that winning percentage.

Two weeks later I woke up about 3:30 A.M. on a Wednesday to the flash of lightning and a rumble of thunder, rain beating wetly on the window. Absolutely the most delicious warmth in the world to be under a down comforter in March in Minnesota with a bitter cold wind driving a hard horizontal rain against the house on a black night lit with sudden blue flashes and the roar of thunder close and all around.

We slid painlessly on into the month that gives us April Fools', another issue-free genuine holiday, requiring guile and imagination—and intimate, because the better the trick, the more it says about the joker's knowledge of the target. By far our most underrated holiday. It should be extended to a week. It comes at such a great time of year, the perfect time for pranks and good humor. We've paid our winter dues and now the sweet promise of spring is fairly knocking our doors down, and we're all optimistic and therefore vulnerable.

But we should make the most of it while we can, before the word *fool* is declared to be negative, perjorative, degrading, judgmental, and marginalizing—do not be surprised at a bill before Congress to have it changed to April Self-Realization Day.

● ● ●

It was a polite winter, that last one of the 1900s. Never raked us unduly, not that I recall, even though a lot of us would have accepted that; and when the time was right it tiptoed out and silently closed the door behind itself. It gave a brief but decent soft snowfall on the eighth of March, snowed all day and into the next morning, tiny flakes building into about a foot or so around here and more in other places. The resulting wet density was perfect for snowballs and that in itself told you to enjoy it because it wouldn't be around very long.

In the middle of April the show pulled up and we went to Peoria, a city named after one of the five tribes of the Illiniwek, rendered *Illinois* by the French and, reading that, you immediately think, So what are the others, Mister Knows It All? and I figured you'd think that so I looked it up for you: They were the Kaskaskia, the Cahokia, the Tamaroa, and the Michigamea.

The downtown was firmly on the ground there, a downtown where most buildings were not only handsome but were as wide as they were tall, and nothing looked like it might tip over. The same might be said about a lot of the people I saw that day. Those weightless sun-dried West Coast types, I didn't see many of them walking around downtown Peoria.

They were quick to point out this was not the Bible Belt here, implying I might have thought so. The city was a recreational hangout for Chicago mobsters during the Prohibition years and they aren't ashamed of the fact. At the S.O.P. Club Thursday night I asked when the music started; I had heard it was a good rockabilly group called the Heatersons. He said, "Oh about eleven-thirty." I thought about that and figured I'd never last that long; had to get up for the early load in. Asked how late they played, he said: "Four." I thought, Minnesota isn't the Bible Belt, either, but it's a lot closer to it than Peoria. Three hours closer, every night. On that downtown block there were nine bars counting the one in the hotel, and they were all doing decent business on a Thursday night.

They sit near the Illinois River with good farmland and oak forest all around, and with easy transportation and a lot of corn they used to barrel more whiskey here than anyplace else in the history of the planet, before or since. The distillery fire is known to be one of the most dramatic manifestations of industrial civilization, and Peoria was the world's best place to find one.

And from dozens of heavy-equipment makers emerged Caterpillar, not only the king of construction machinery but my choice as builders of the best truck engines as well. And Keystone Steel & Wire was, in the late 1930s, the largest independent steel and wire fence mill in the world; they had one machine that did nothing but make fencing for the King Ranch in Texas, over two thousand miles of it. They also sponsored the famous *WLS Barn Dance,* broadcast live from Chicago.

Got back to Minnesota just in time to enjoy Severe Weather Awareness Week here, the television weatherpersons' version of Mardi Gras. They had been just explaining their little asses off all week, beaming and radiant with every nuance of cold fronts and inversions. The bottom line is always the same, of course: Go down to the basement. Probably a lot of viewers go down to their basements just to watch the weather news.

We are heavy into awareness and understanding in Minnesota, if anybody hasn't noticed. The coming spring and summer will no doubt bring Wide Load Awareness Week, Open Manhole Vigilance Week, Protective Eyewear Understanding Week, Sunburn Cognizance Days, Tick And Flea Comprehension Week, and Stray Dog Awareness Month. Cold-weather celebrations may include Slippery Streets Discernment Week, Black Ice Heedfulness Week, and Thin Ice Consciousness Month. In my adopted state we also appreciate and discover. We look forward to events like Heimlich Maneuver Appreciation Day and Neighborhood Hazards Discovery Week.

I took a breakfast ride on an April Monday out to the country where the soil lay ready for seed and heat. There was a light spray in the air, so light we seemed to be getting wet without discomfort of rain or even fog; kind of like those misting pipes they have under the awnings in San Antonio sidewalk cafes to cool the summer evenings. It was a most excellent quiet spring morning.

The fields were neat, orderly, each in its own state of readiness. Some sat in a short light green buzz cut of alfalfa or timothy or clover, and seemed eager to get on with growing up; others waited in cleanly manicured dirt, free of mark or vegetation, harrowed smooth and open to any suggestion. Some fields held Roman legions of light beige corn stubble, rough hewn but holding ranks, and still others were in sensuous fluid rows of fresh-turned black. All were locked in place by woods, the birch and aspen showing a downy pale green fuzz, the oaks still dark and skeptical against their exuberance.

It's the other way around, of course: The fields are holding the woods back. The woods are itching to march. Left unattended those fields would be weeds in a year and forest in a decade. It happened over nine years in my backyard in northeast Minneapolis, as under benign renter neglect the white man's green lawn became first a chest-high tangle of burning weed and thistle and then emerged a few years later as a small but leafy Indian forest. I drove by there last summer and there were tall trees in the backyard, standing in tribute to my laziness. If we stopped farming I assume most of the state would be soon covered with trees.

A stranger driving that farm country would sense no hint of the farm crisis suspended over it all, nothing to suggest that farmers were gathered by the hundreds in a South St. Paul hotel for a meeting. They came from Texas, Colorado, Ohio, Wisconsin, Iowa, Nebraska, the Dakotas, Kansas, for the Midwest Farm Crisis Forum. Behind the speakers hung large posters on their Wall of Shame, posters of Cargill, Land O'Lakes, Archer Daniels Midland, ConAgra. They wanted the government to stand up and keep the manipulators of the markets from sucking them dry. Our senators were there and did some vigorous talking but offered no solution. Two federal officials were there and promised nothing. Jesse Ventura and Bill Clinton took identical positions on this issue, mouthing words of sincere sympathy and doing nothing about it.

In a full cafe I sat next to an old man who, after the usual introductory weather talk, said, "I will have to say the longer things go on the worse it gets and you don't have to look very far to see it neither because, tarnation, they can't even make a decent hot turkey sandwich anymore, all you get is that sliced turkey loaf in there, you don't get real turkey, I mean it might be stuff that's from a turkey but it's not the real meat, and that gravy they make now is nothin' but flavored glue and the bread ain't real bread neither, nothin' like it used to be, it's all limp. I could make better bread. Anybody could.

"And these cars now, they got plastic bumpers and you look under the hood and you don't even see the engine, all you see is plumbing and tubing and little skinny wires and there's no way a guy can change plugs or points or none of that stuff, you're lucky if you can even check the oil these days, never mind tryna change the oil or the filter or anything, and when I was a kid we thought nothing of changing a whole engine or a transmission or whatever, like me and Gilbert Norris, hell, we took the tranny out of his 'forty-one Ford and put in one we got at the junkyard for twenty bucks, dang good tranny, took us two days is all, just kids, and he drove that thing for ten years after that and it still ran good when he sold it."

I nodded. He continued. "Sold it to a guy one time when we were on the way up north to go fishing, this guy saw the car and said, Man, a 'forty-one Ford coupe, that's my all-time favorite car, and he offered Gilbert twice what that car was worth and Gil said You got a deal but we were goin' fishin first. We caught our limits that day, big walleyes and some northerns, too, and he sold that old car to the guy on the way back. But y'know, the cars like that are long gone. Antiques, now. Showpieces. Not really cars, 'cause they're too precious. And the fishin' ain't that good anymore, neither. Well, I gotta be goin'. I got a shelf I need to hang." He got up and left so he wouldn't have to listen to my particular beef. Whatever it may have been that day, he was fairly sure he didn't want to hear it. He left while he was ahead.

The old men on the other side of me talked of fishing also, but in the present tense. The near one said the crappies were biting pretty good for a while yesterday but then not so good, even though they were still around. Couldn't get 'em to go for those small minnows. The other said, "Harvey seemed to be having good luck lately using a little Rapala, just a little thing."

"Well I never thought of that," said the first. He pondered it for a while. "How would you cast a thing like that? Too light to get anywhere with regular rod and reel, I suppose. Maybe a guy would have to use a fly rod or something because you couldn't hang a weight on there—it just wouldn't work right, would it?"

"No, prob'ly not, but with crappies I don't think you'd have to cast all that far anyways. Just flip it out there a ways and bring it back in, y'know, kinda wiggle it up and down so she looks like she's swimming, I guess. He seemed to be having some luck anyways—that's what he told me. I'm not even sure I'm gonna believe it, until I try it."

"Well. I always figured if they wouldn't bite on real minnows they wouldn't bite on anything, but heck, I'd sure try it. A rig like that would save a lot of foolin' around with the minnows."

"Ya, a guy could try it for a while, and if it don't work you can always go back to the minnows. Sunnies, they'll be bitin' pretty soon too. I don't mind them small fish, y'know? It's somethin' to do until walleye season, anyways."

"Well that's right," said the first guy. I got the feeling they held this ritual conversation, or some version of it, nearly every weekday.

Their hands were gnarled like the roots of trees along a shoreline. The fingers wavered slightly around the doughnut but were lock-tight around the thick white walls of the coffee cup as the waitress poured the refill. I ordered the number four and decaf coffee. "Decaf?" She looked at me as if I had blurted it out by mistake. I nodded. She said, "Instant okay?"

I got the message. "Just give me the regular. I'd rather have that anyway." She smiled, pleased to relieve me of my brief madness.

The cafe hadn't changed much in the last thirty years; the dark wood back cabinet and shelves with the stainless-steel Rheinhart five-burner coffeemaker there, not all that stainless anymore; the double-spout KoldMilk cabinet with the heavy counterweight dispensing knobs, a pressed plastic glue-on strip sign that read, CUT MILK TUBE AT 45 DEGREE ANGLE. Both white plastic tubes hanging beneath were cut straight across at ninety degrees; hard to say if it was out of defiance or indifference. No pies or anything else in the sloped-glass display boxes on the counter but a pile of doughnuts back next to the coffee machine.

You have to like a place that doesn't have decaf coffee. Not all the guys in that rural restaurant were geezers but most weren't much younger than forty. They've all had the mortgage, most are orphaned, they've all been badgered by banks and battered by bad times. An accumulation of numberless disasters in that little cafe: falls, crashes, cuts, burns, foreclosures, lost children, bankruptcies, divorces, bypasses, tumors, hernias; fingers cut off, bones broken, discs ruptured, joints dislocated, ligaments torn; stepped on by cattle, thrown by horses, kicked by mules. Hundreds of years in the blazing sun and bitter cold accrued here, weathered men with deep-wrinkled foreheads who have paid their dues and who now sip coffee and talk quietly about catching sunfish. Small talk and deliberately so, without issue or importance, the conversation an end unto itself.

5

THE STUNT BABY AND THE RUNAWAY

WE ENDED OUR SEASON THAT JUNE 1999 with a trip to four historic interior cities, starting with Butte and then doing Greeley, Reno, and Knoxville. The ride on I–94 out through North Dakota was lush and green, prairie stretching off into a fine haze: little dots of cattle way out there. In a blue-black near-darkness after sundown, a pond in the western hills reflected the sky brighter than the sky itself; it was as if the pond was lit from below, an iridescent blue glowing in the dark, surrounded by shapes of buffalo. I slept in the truck near the border. In the morning the moodiness of western Dakota yielded to the drama of Montana's very large sky and later to its mountains, rising to the Continental Divide from whose heights you descend directly into Butte.

I generally look forward to the music towns—Memphis, Nashville, New Orleans, Kansas City, Austin, San Antonio, Fort Worth—but I also have to admit an overriding weakness for anyplace in Montana. And especially for Butte, and not only because my brother moved out there thirty years ago and that it sits directly over the mines, but for the spirit and the sheer stubborn funkiness of the place. It is a city where beer and liquor were openly served day and night during the entire thirteen-year non-sense of Prohibition and where the sound of exploding dynamite was for decades considered the Sound of Money. A city with a fabulous history, once rich and opulent and now with the largest man-made hole in the world right in the middle of it, a hole that had yielded up a third of the world's copper and is now filling up with mineral water—minerals like mercury—making it one of the world's great Superfund cleanup projects. The city was home to Evel Knievel, the motorcycle daredevil who was at one time up for consideration by the state legislature to be named the State Bird of Montana.

We loaded into the refurbished Mother Lode Theater on Friday morning, with a crew that was glad to see us in town. In these smaller cities the stagehands never comment on the fact we are just a one-truck show. They don't mention things like Vince Gill coming in with eight semis. I bought chains once at a truck supply house in St. Paul for a winter run out to the West Coast and was told I got the last set; the Rolling Stones had been there that week and had bought sixteen sets for sixteen semis.

That afternoon I found myself with time to kill and walked a couple of blocks and around the corner to the

Silver Dollar Saloon and ended up sitting a couple of stools away from a man watching a baseball game. He was wearing jeans and a western shirt, no hat, probably in his later forties. I ordered a beer and the two of us sat there viewing the screen, detached, as if we were watching gulls on a pier.

A runner was measuring his jump off first base, hands low, a skinny guy that you knew was a speed merchant or else he wouldn't be in the game. The right-handed batter pulled a screaming liner, short-hopped outside the third baseman, right on the line, a ball that would have sent an ordinary human sprawling, and he spun and backhanded it low and came up throwing, a blur, whipping it to second, where it was taken in midair and shot on to first like a signal off a microwave tower. "Shee-iitt!" I blurted out in spite of myself.

The guy looked at me with a wry smile, nodding his head once sideways and pursing his lips in the *ain't-that-something* gesture. We watched the replay, first in slow motion and then in real time, and I said, "I've seen alley cats that were slow compared to those two guys."

"Yeah. That was pretty."

The play ended the inning with the score tied at two, and they replayed it again when they came back from the commercial. It was a double play at the extreme end of the genre: a fast runner with a good jump, the ball on the third-base line and deep. A lot of players would have settled for the out at first—and even that wasn't a given, nasty as the ball was hit. We watched without saying anything more, neither wanting to seem too friendly. Finally I said, "I bet not one guy in ten thousand could have made that play."

He thought for second. "Probably closer to one in a hundred thousand."

"Yeah. That'd be more like it."

After another pause I said, "How big you think this whole state is?"

"Maybe a little under a million. Nine hundred thousand."

"So let's just say five hundred thousand are guys, and if even one guy in a hundred thousand could do it, that'd be five guys in this state who could make that play. And I doubt it."

"Well, three of those five'd be either too young or too old, right? So there'd be maybe two guys."

"Right. But I doubt even two. Maybe one. Maybe one guy in the whole state of Montana could do that."

The bartender asked if he wanted another and he said yeah and nodded casually at my beer. I thanked him and he didn't say anything. After a couple of outs and a walk and a hit he said, "Y'know, if you think of all the millions in the country, what is it, two hundred eighty million,

something like that, and if one out of every million popu-
lation could make that play that's two hundred eighty in
the whole country that could do it. But I bet there's not
even twenty, on all the major league teams, who could
come up with that ball and make that throw."

"Yeah. It's true. Amazing what some of these guys can
do. People get bored when they see it so much. They don't
think that much about it."

The visitors' half of the inning ended on a deep fly ball
to center field and we talked about sports for a while, not
so much about the teams but about the stars, Michael Jordan, Muhammad Ali, Ozzie Smith. Jerry Rice. I said, "The
thing about football, and even more so in boxing, is that
while you're doing all this amazing stuff some other guy
about the same size is trying to punish hell out of you. I
mean it takes a lot of courage to do some of this stuff. And
baseball players, too, looking at a ninety-five-mile-an-hour
fastball—I'd be thinkin' no-thank-you-very-much."

He said, "In the major leagues, you either have the
reflexes and the eyesight or you don't, and they find out
real quick."

"Right. And any one play goes wrong, and suddenly the
whole career is kaput . . . and like these Hollywood stunt-
men, too. That jumping off high places makes my hands
sweat. Man. Like nightmares."

"Oh yeah?"

"Oh yeah. I look down from a balcony on the twentieth floor of a hotel and I think I might jump; the edge of that rail is like a magnet."

He sat there quiet, in a way that invited questioning. "So you've done some of that?" I asked.

He said, "Yeah," sort of guarded. "A few times."

"So you're like a skydiver or something?"

He thought about it. "Something like that. Only I was a stunt baby."

"What. A stunt baby? I never heard of a stunt baby."

"Yeah. Back in the crazy times in the films, when they were doing those snuff movies in South America . . . and all that other real edgy, over-the-line stuff. They used me for a stunt baby."

"Never heard of such a thing. They'd like throw you?"

"Throw me. Yeah, I'll say. They'd drop me off cliffs. Out of tall buildings. Stunts like that. You ever hear of a director named Adrian Blood?"

"No; I don't know. Maybe."

"He made underground films; he'd do things that'd just make people scream. He was a pioneer in the violence thing. He'd do these low-budget movies and sell 'em to rich people for their private little showings. Couldn't do any of this in public, even back then; I mean it was way out there. Sicko, whacko; the kind of thing you could get busted for."

"You have these movies?"

"Yeh. Some of 'em. There'd be some scene with this little angel-face child, beautiful smile, a cherub, you couldn't help but just want to pick 'im up and hold him, and they go to the cliffs along the seashore, the family, and old Grandpa is carrying him along the high rocky pathway and he slips and then, y'know, off camera, the director hollers bring the stunt baby and the next thing there I am, sailing through the air, falling two hundred feet into a net. But of course you don't see the net. But they get three camera angles, me flying out of his hands from above and from below, and from the side. I'm just kinda movin' my arms and legs and my eyes get real big, and I mean you can tell it's not a dummy or anything. People would practically wet their pants. Sometimes they'd faint."

"Wow."

"Yeah. And it wasn't about me, the baby, it's about the old man. What does he do now, how does he deal with it? He drops his little grandson to his death; who can live after that? That was like the message of the film. But, you know, it was mainly just a way to scare the hell out of people. Another time they dropped me off a balcony, just like you said, twenty stories, straight down."

"So do you remember any of this?"

"Oh yeah. Probably not the earliest stuff, but they did this till I was about four or five and I can remember a lot of it. One time the kid was kidnapped by a bad biker dude and they take off and the cops chase 'em and they go out in the country and there's a barn burning and they put me on there, on the motorcycle seat in front of the guy, and we drive right through this burning barn, in one door and out the other. I remember that one really well. Now they do that trick on the computer."

"Man."

"And then there were the parties. We lived in Beverly Hills and they'd have these crazy parties, and somewhere along the way somebody'd say 'Bring out the stunt baby' and next thing I knew I'd be falling off the diving board, or off the roof onto a trampoline, or some other goofy thing."

"Wow . . . So your parents, they thought nothing of this? This was obviously all right with them, I mean, they probably—"

"Oh sure. They'd throw me up in the air when I was real little and I'd laugh. I think that's how they got the idea."

"So they knew this director guy?"

"Well, they *were* this director guy. Adrian Blood was my dad. But of course that wasn't his real name. My mother and him, they believed everything is meant to happen anyway, and they really believed it, so you know, I mean if something bad happened, that was just the way it was supposed to go down. And it probably wasn't as bad as it sounds. They used a pretty big net, and I'd fall like a ham."

Not much to say to a story like that one. I bought a round and asked where it all had led—if he'd later worked as a stuntman or an actor or anything. He said no, that he had a strange childhood and the money he made that was supposed to be in a trust didn't amount to much and he left home at seventeen and became a construction roustabout. Worked on oil rigs, electric transmission towers, radio towers. Never afraid of heights. Said his dad was a real jerk when you got right down to it and his mother "went off the deep end."

He said: "A lot of my friends with parents in the movie business got all messed up, too much money, too much attention. Christ they'd be in analysis and they'd have their own astrologers and all that crap. My father never reached the real big money but everybody knew who he was and he had a certain status. But I just split as soon as I could. It was a weird existence. My mother was zoned out most of the time; some days she hardly knew me and other days she was maudlin as hell. I got out. Couple years after that my dad crashed his plane in Brazil."

I'm sitting there wondering what he's doing sitting in this bar watching baseball and I'm thinking that for a guy with a strange childhood he seems to be doing okay, maybe not great but pretty normal anyway, and then in walks this right-from-Central-Casting drop-dead beauty in tight jeans: black hair, tall, radiant, perfect teeth, lights up the whole room, comes right up to the guy and gives him a big smooch and asks if he's been waiting long and he says It's always too long when I'm waiting for you honey and they finally turn to me and make some polite small talk and then they disappear, the Beauty and the Stunt Baby. I mentioned our show the next night and hoped they'd drop by but they never did.

That night my brother gave me an insider's tour of some down-to-earth hangouts, even though he had quit drinking years before, and in the Helsinki Bar and Sauna up on the hill in Finntown a gentleman he knew told us a story about a Minnesota fellow who went out there way back in the old days. I had to infer some of the details here, but I got telephone help later from the man's granddaughter Eleanor, back in Minnesota.

Nels Rasmusson was born in rural Minnesota in 1886 to Norwegian immigrants, hardworking farmers who cleared land and plowed with horses and came to make a good living. He was the youngest of six, with three brothers, Carl, Joseph, and Albert, and two sisters, Elaine and Beatrice.

He went to school, helped on the farm, cut wood, and played an accordion given to him by his favorite uncle, who could no longer play because of arthritis; and when it came time to choose a life's work he hesitated. Farming was not unpleasant but it wasn't exciting to him either. He took a job at a machinery company and sold steam tractors and plows and cultivators, but his heart wasn't in sales. He liked to dance and play music and have fun, and he liked to drink beer. His next-older brother Albert had moved to Minneapolis, and they carried on a thirty-year correspondence in Norwegian. When Albert passed on in 1972 the boxes full of letters were given to Nels's son Marvin, who is now himself in his eighties, and it was Marvin's daughter Eleanor who had the letters translated and was able to reconstruct this story of her grandfather's secret adventure in the West.

In 1911, at the age of twenty-five, Nels met a man in a tavern near the train station in Little Falls, a middle-aged fellow passing through on his way back to Butte. "It's the richest hill on earth," the man said. He had traveled to Minneapolis "just for the sheer hell of it. They got stuff down there you wouldn't believe. Look at this watch." He pulled out a luxurious gold pocket watch, made in

London. He said, "You should see the pistol I bought there. Engraved; made in France. Ivory grips. You wouldn't believe it."

Nels wondered how the man got his money but didn't have to ask. "I worked in the mines in Butte. I had a share of a silver mine there, before the silver crash in 1893 and I sold before it went down. Started out as a miner and saved a little money and bought mining stocks. They'd go up and I'd sell. After the silver crash people thought Butte mining was done for, but I knew it hadn't even started. A few guys knew they were sitting on a huge copper deposit but they didn't say much about it. They bought up old silver mines, and I bought a couple myself. When the copper got going I sold again; one mine I bought and sold twice. First for silver and then for copper. The first man sold it when it ran out of gold, in 1887, and I got it cheap."

Nels was interested. The man talked on. "Butte right now is the most exciting city in the world. There are carnivals, parades, baseball, ice cream parlors; ten different theaters, shows from New York, Chicago, biggest names in show business, whatever you want to see. High-class taverns, women everywhere; there's twenty dance halls in that town. Streets are packed with people. People of all races, from all over the world. The most beautiful buildings you can imagine. The new courthouse has a stained-glass dome; you'd think you were in Europe somewhere."

Nels thought about that. Women. Excitement.

"There's a whole city underground, too, and not just the mines. The downtown is all connected by tunnels, and there's stores and little cafes and everything you could ask for, all underneath the streets. And a lot of people don't know a thing about it. It's sort of a local secret. It's an amazing place."

Nels asked if there were jobs out there still. "It's booming more now than ever. You ride into town in the morning and by that night you've put in a full day's work. Nothing to it."

"In the mines, too?"

"Oh yes. I'll give you my card and I guarantee you'll be working in a day. I know the foreman at the Speculator Mine personally. He'll put you to work, and he'll make sure you get your pay on time, too. You look me up when you come out." The card said DANIEL MCCHESNEY—INVEST-MENTS; he wrote the Speculator foreman's name on the back.

Nels told his family he was going out west for an adventure, but he wanted to make a life out there. Heady times for a young man at the beginning of the industrial revolution; something new almost every month. Farm tractors, automobiles, locomotives, photography, radio, electricity. He wanted to be someplace where the pace was fast but it wasn't crowded; somewhere out west.

He took his accordion and a suitcase and went to Butte and found it all to be true; rented a room and located McChesney and was working in a copper mine the second day he was in town. They worked three shifts a day, eight hours each. He was on the second shift and would come out at midnight and go downtown to eat and find himself in the middle of a huge crowd, the city lit up and having a great time.

The labor was pitiless. He had worked on threshing crews, on timber crews, and none of it had prepared him for the darkness, the damp, the smoke, the claustrophobic tunnels, the sheer pace and roughness of it all. Most miners were Welsh, Irish, Cornish, or Italian; he was out of place. He held tough for a time. He figured a Norwegian could be just as stubborn as any of these fellows, until the incident one day involving a man named Miller.

He'd been there three months and still didn't know anyone very well. Miller worked two shifts, first and second, every day. One shift was exhausting enough for Nels and he thought this man must be insane to put in two. They were working close together when a large boulder dislodged from the wall beside Miller and rolled, cleanly snapping his lower leg with a cracking sound like a ship's mast breaking. Miller went down without the amount of screaming you might expect from a break like that and lay pinned beneath the rock. They rigged a chain and a couple of pry bars so they could lift the stone and the foreman sent him topside with two helpers and the rest went back to work loading mucking cars with ore.

The next day Nels was stunned to find Miller back at work, a little slow but pretty much as if nothing had happened. He didn't know him well enough to grill him about the doctor and what he had done but he figured it was splinted and plastered and hurt like hell—and if that's what it took to be a miner then he should probably find some other line of work. When he drew his pay that week he thanked the man for the experience and said he had enjoyed it very much but that he needed to be outside, and thanks again.

Two days later he heard about the hoist running out of control at the Leonard mine and dropping five men fifteen hundred feet to their deaths. Nels felt lucky to be leaving the mining trade still alive and in one piece.

He was soon working on a Scandinavian logging crew. There was a lot of wood to be cut up there in the mountains. Some of the men spoke Norwegian. The work was as rough as mining but at least they were outside in the light and the fresh air. After he'd been there about two months he made what he thought was a humorous remark about an older Norwegian's backside and the fellow came over and knocked him down with a hard left hook. He got up and asked what the hell that was for and got knocked down again, this time with the right, costing him a tooth. As the youngest of four farm boys, Nels thought he could fight. He got up again and hit the old man as hard as he could in the ribs and got knocked down a third time. This routine went on for a while, until he could find no sensible reason to continue and began to wonder if he would ever be able to eat solid food again. When he drew his pay he thanked the man for the experience and said he was looking for something a little different from logging. But thank you.

He took his money and went to the dance halls, where he asked musicians if anyone knew of a band in need of an accordion player. He was soon playing schottisches and waltzes and polkas seven nights a week, mostly for people so drunk they barely knew their own names. The money wasn't all that great but it was a living and the work was more fun than mining or logging. And he was finally beginning to enjoy his western adventure.

And then he met Audrey. She came to a dance one night and seemed to take a real liking to him. She was shy and very pretty and on their third meeting came up to his room late at night with a bottle of brandy. He became very drowsy after one drink and when he woke up Audrey was gone and so was his arthritic uncle's accordion and he never saw either again. Although someone in the band, when Nels told him what had happened, said that Audrey was a lady who normally worked down in "the district" and was not as shy as she may have seemed.

He got a job as a waiter in a fine restaurant, purely by chance, a job for which he had no aptitude at all and lasted only until the third day, when he tilted a plate of roast beef, mashed potatoes, gravy, and peas over the shoulder and into the lap of a mining executive entertaining his investors, and a brief fifteen minutes later dropped a tray of desserts and aperitifs onto another table laden full with wineglasses and cups of coffee. A shocking loud explosion in the center of a party of six. All were horrified, including of course the manager, who fired him right there at the table.

He enrolled in a two-week bartending school, where they guaranteed a job on graduation and you could sign away half your first month's earnings to pay for tuition. His first job was in a bar frequented by Scandinavians, and sure as hell the old Norwegian who had given him such a rough time on the logging crew came in and had a few aquavits and recognized him and reached over the bar and took a swing at him and missed and Nels popped the old man a good one and then nailed him again just for old times' sake and in the grand melee that followed half the liquor bottles in the place were broken and the other half disappeared out the door. And Nels had a broken left wrist.

The owner had been beside him when it started but was bent down into a cooler and didn't see the first swing; all he saw was his polite new employee fresh from bartender school grab an old man by the front of the shirt and slug him twice in the kisser, whereupon the old man's relatives proceeded to trash his bar and a few of his regulars as well. Nels didn't dare ask for his pay. He went instead to a hospital where they put a cast on the wrist.

He walked the town for a while and came upon the livery stables where the carriages were kept. He had been around horses on the farm and there was a demand for hack drivers, even one in a cast. They rented him an outfit, including a black top hat, and he met Fat Jack Jones, the internationally known hack driver who drove kings and presidents, actresses and athletes, and all the famous people who came to Butte.

He ran into his friend McChesney while he was waiting for a fare outside one of the opulent downtown establishments. McChesney asked what he'd been up to and when he told him about the incident in the mine with Miller, McChesney said: "Miller is sort of famous around here. He went swimming in a flooded pit when he was sixteen years old. Cut his leg on a sharp piece of metal underwater and he got an infection that got so bad they had to cut the leg off. He's got a wooden leg. And he has another wooden leg, his better one, that he keeps at home. He's working two shifts to save money to open a boot store."

Well, that explains it, Nels thought.

He had been hoping to save enough money himself to have McChesney show him how to get rich with it, but things kept happening. Two weeks later and before his wrist had healed he chanced to be at the railroad depot on a summer Thursday evening as Fat Jack Jones met the Norwegian ambassador, in town for an official visit. He was the next hack in line and was given two of the ambassador's aides to take to their posh downtown hotel. He was suddenly filled with Norwegian pride and a great feeling of good fortune at having so important a mission, but as he pulled away from the depot a sudden explosion, a large firecracker or a dynamite cap, or even a pistol shot, he never knew which, spooked the horse. It reared up and then took off running, and having only one hand for control he was unable to get the animal to slow down.

He was hanging on to the reins out of desperation, surprised that this well-mannered horse was tearing hell-bent through the crowded streets of the city completely out of control. They went uphill to the city center and slid around a corner and sideswiped an ice wagon, sending Nels's top hat flying into the crowd, and then were hurled around the next corner where they bounced off a lamppost. They were now dashing back down the steep hill on

Montana Street with a loose wheel and his passengers frozen in fear. The horse was heading for the stable but the wheel fell off before they got there, and the hack went into a long and terrible downhill skid on its side, throwing Nels to the street. A reporter was on him almost before he stopped sliding.

The passengers were bruised and shaken but not injured. The carriage was salvageable; Nels had a dislocated shoulder and some abrasions. The worst part was the story in the paper, exaggerated for humor and drama, tagging him with the name "Runaway Rasmusson, the Flying Norwegian."

He wrote his brother Albert:

Sunday, August 11, 1912

Had a most unhappy experience leaving the railroad station Friday. . . . [He described the accident.] This latest incident has discouraged me greatly. I seem not a good fit with this place. Am considering a return to Minnesota but perhaps tomorrow things will change. Much happens in this city and blind circumstance seems to rule the lives of the inhabitants; some die, some survive, with pure chance being the sole arbiter of the fate of each. Give my regards to the family.

Your brother Nels.

He had an arm in a sling and a cast on a wrist and a face full of scrapes and discouragement. He owed money for his lost hat and the ruined outfit. He was behind on his rent, owed for groceries, and had only three dollars in his pocket. He went back to the dance hall and found the band he had been with, the only friends he had managed to meet, and sat and drank five-cent beers and listened to polkas and schottisches. They said they had read about him in the paper, about him being famous now: Fat Jack Jones and Runaway Rasmusson. It stung.

A well-dressed woman with a knowing look sat next to him and said, "You used to play in this band, didn't you?"

He ended up at her house and she took good care of him. (If this were real fiction, here is where the steamy sex scene would happen. We will only speculate on the level of steaminess here, but apparently it was sufficient.) He picked up his meager belongings at the rooming house and moved in. By the last week of September both the wrist and the shoulder were healed and her husband was due back from Philadelphia. She hadn't mentioned the husband and he hadn't asked but assumed there probably was one, given the opulence of her surroundings. She gave him twenty dollars one morning and bid him a teary farewell at her back doorstep.

He wrote his brother: ". . . She was the nicest and sweetest woman I ever met. I think I shall never find another like her—it would be too great a favor to ask of fate."

A twenty then would resemble a thousand these days. He would gamble half and if he won he would take the train back to Minnesota, and if he lost he would stay in Butte and make the best of it on the remaining ten. He was a good enough poker player and it wasn't hard to find a game; the trick, he figured, was to find one where he could win and walk out.

He went into the underground city. In the back of a small diner was a gaming room frequented by miners. Whiskey was available. He had a chance there, he thought; the high rollers and the card sharks and thieves preferred the faster action up in the fancy hotels and taverns.

And in the end it all rested on the turn of a single card, as it did in movies yet unfilmed and novels yet unwritten. They were playing five-card stud, a brutal game dealt one card facedown and four cards faceup to each, one at a time, a round of betting after each one. No wild cards, no common cards, no chance to improve the five you're dealt. Seven players and a house dealer sitting at a round table with a green felt cover, a game of nerve, for purists, with an ordinary pair or even a single ace often enough to win the hand.

After three hours he was still holding about even, bluffing just enough to plant the idea, and waiting for a string of luck. He won a couple of decent hands in a row and after four cards in the next deal he held a king in the hole with another king showing, usually an easy winner, but around the table he was looking at a possible spade flush with an ace up, a possible jack-high straight, and a pair of nines and an ace coupled to what must be another ace down, or even a nine, the way its owner was betting; and in the middle, because of the four good hands, the largest pot of the night.

They bet around again and he was sweating bullets, thinking he would be stuck in Butte for the rest of his life, a city where he just didn't fit, and then an amazing last card sailed from the dealer's fingers across the pot and landed before him, the king of clubs, holding a broadsword; he flew in and seemed to say "I'm here to help, son." The straight didn't hit and he dropped but the rest kept raising. The spade flush turned out to be just a pair of aces and the nines also had an ace in the hole. A big two pair like aces and nines, they make a person bet like mad—but they don't beat three kings.

He scooped up the pile and left behind a table of surly miners wanting to kill him, went and packed, paid his rent, paid the owner of the hack for the lost top hat, and walked down to the depot with seventy-eight fat dollars in his pocket. Runaway Rasmusson, the Flying Norwegian.

Years afterward when people would ask him about his

days in Montana he'd say, "Well, it's real pretty out there, but y'know, a guy gets used to somethin' and a lot of times he'll come back to it, even if it isn't the most interesting thing in the world. You have to go with what's comfortable." He wouldn't say much more than that. Never gave out the details of how his life's course had been changed by a king with a sword, and Albert never said much either.

And, incidentally, Miller's Shoe Store is still open in Butte and still in the family. I know this because my brother married Miller's granddaughter.

6

THE LONELIEST ROAD IN AMERICA

I LEFT FOR GREELEY SUNDAY MORNING after the Butte show, starting with a hefty pull up over the Continental Divide and then having an easy time of it from there on east on I–90 and south on I–25. The site of the Battle of the Little Bighorn is just off the freeway at Crow Agency, where the famous shutout by the Indians was won in the summer of 1876. It happened just a week after Wild Bill Hickock was shot in the head in Deadwood and seven weeks after the first major-league no-hitter was pitched, by George Bradley of the St. Louis Brown Stockings, against the Hartford Dark Blues. Seems like a long way for a team to travel to play baseball in those days.

Took US 85 into Colorado, through small farm towns like Eaton, and when I got there I did a little snooping around and found that Greeley was originally intended to be utopia. The editor of the *New York Tribune*, Horace Greeley, sent his ag editor out west with these words, among others:

*. . . Now I desire and am in earnest for human-
ity's sake that you people build up an asylum
under the shadow of the Rocky Mountains, under
new circumstances, where you will live by irrigation and flourish in a new clime, where a man can
go and cannot get drunk. . . . There are many
places in the world where you can go to get drunk
but very few where you are obliged to keep sober.*

The guy had been out there in 1869 and went back with
the notion of building a temperate, nonindustrial agrarian
utopia in the new lands (new to them anyway), notwith-
standing that there already was a utopian nonindustrial
temperate society in place out there, at least there was
until the cavalry came along.

But it wasn't just temperance they were after. The grand
vision saw religion, education, agriculture, irrigation,
cooperation, family values, high moral standards, and
money. One hundred eighty dollars bought you a plot of
land and membership in the Union Colony. But booze and
the Law of Unintended Consequences are powerful
forces, and they manifested themselves unto Greeley
when small single-street bar towns, Evans, Rosedale, and
Garden City, grew on the southern border of town. Greeley, "The Athens of the West," became to some "Eaton on
the north and Drinkin' on the south."

And they had another funny problem. They had to put a fence around the city because it sat on the main cattle route between Wyoming and Texas, and all those steers, hell, they just walked right through the place. And that didn't change much after they put the fence in either, because barbed wire hadn't been invented yet and those steers—well, you know how they are. Kinda big and singleminded. Ranchers called it a "spite fence" and dubbed Greeley the "City of Saints" or "City of Hayseeds and High Morals," with a fence to keep the sinners out.

It's a darn nice place now, with a college and parks and boulevards, a stone courthouse, a civic center and a museum, trees, and all the rest of it. But they still have a lot of cattle in town. Big holding pens on the northeast, a billion-dollar industry that doesn't smell that good when the wind is wrong. Luckily the wind is usually right. And of course the wind doesn't matter to cattlemen, who call that perfume the Smell of Money.

I headed for Reno the Sunday morning after the show, north to Cheyenne and west, thinking I'd gladly drive Wyoming for free if I could get double pay for some other places.

And as beautiful as it all was you wouldn't call it lush, and it seemed odd to drive westward across the progressively more spare and rocky landscape of Nevada to finally slip through the green valley of the Truckee River and arrive at the abrupt assemblage of overactive neon that is Reno; as if the 750 miles of mountains, plains, and foothills all the way back to Cheyenne had been raked clean of sound and color and it all got dragged up there against the Sierra Nevadas. Straddling two freeways, crossed by mainline railroad tracks and a rushing river and unfettered by convention, it is a hotbed of gaudy activity, awash in colored light from ten thousand blinking slot machines singing in *boops* and *beeps* like one giant merry-go-round, rattling with the constant metal-to-metal *chink-chink-chink-chink* of coins dropping into stainless-steel trays. Most of the time those ladies scoop 'em all up and feed 'em back in. In Reno, of course, the Sound of Money *is* money. Some of those quarters must spend their entire lives waiting in stacks and falling through the same slot machines, never seeing the inside of a cowboy's pocket or resting on an old mahogany bar, not to mention the warm joy of being wrapped in the moist grip of some little kid.

It has a remarkable history, this area from here down to Virginia City. They took four thousand tons of gold out of there in twenty-five years, part of which financed the Union in the Civil War. The South likely had no idea of what they were up against; it was more gold than the entire world had dug up in the previous 350 years. It was also the world's center for technology; in 1870, drilling three thousand feet into the earth was the engineering equivalent of going to the moon.

The place was named after Jesse Reno, a major general in the Union army who was killed in the Battle of South Mountain and who never set foot in the city. The downtown is small and easily walked, and in the bright midday heat I toured some casinos, popped out one air door and back in the next, from one cool dark mirrored sanctuary into another. And in every casino a slot machine was always, somewhere in its undefined landscape, clattering out a jackpot. In the gift shop of the hotel I found, amid the trinkets and T-shirts and toothpaste, twenty-four-hour fifths of whiskey and directories for Nevada brothels. It was the opposite of Minnesota, the state where you can do nearly nothing and what you can do they tell you when; in Nevada you can do almost anything and do it anytime you please. You can get married at a drive-through chapel as easily as picking up a couple of Whoppers, and you can get divorced faster than you can sell the car.

Our venue was at the University of Nevada, directly north of the downtown. After a smooth load-in on Friday morning I went to a local truck stop and fueled up and had coffee. Asked the driver next to me at the counter about US 50 back through the middle of Nevada; he told me it's the loneliest road in America. That might be just fine, I said, and another driver said you gotta be careful out there, it's open range. He said one time he hit a full-grown bull.

That'd get your attention wouldn't it, I said, and he replied that it totaled his truck and trailer both when they went into the ditch and jackknifed, and on top of that the farmer said it was his prize bull, worth six thousand dollars. But where he hit it in Kansas wasn't open range; the bull had come through a little single-strand wire fence. The sheriff told him later: "That bull weren't no more prize animal than I am." The insurance never did pay for the bull and neither did he.

I figured I could take my chances with open-range bulls and it would be no problem to take a two-lane road for four hundred miles of the twenty-three-hundred-mile trip to Knoxville. Especially if it's the loneliest road in America. And in fact it was terrific out there on US 50. A hundred miles between towns. A sign pointed down a dusty side road going off to what looked like nowhere: It said RATTLESNAKE SPEEDWAY. Passed a small place called Salt Wells, one rambling building and two small trees by the road, desert in all directions, with a couple of neon beer signs and a big sign that said GIRLS. Three pickup trucks parked in front. I know what you're thinking but I didn't stop in. Not even in the interest of research.

The sign for open range is a black silhouette of a bull,

horns high, tail swinging; they post it about every ten miles. Every bull along a ninety-mile stretch there had a bullet hole through the heart, one shot in each, same place every time. Looked impressive. I wondered if it was somebody with a grudge against the highway department or maybe an aggravated bull rider, and was it done once a week like a careful body of work, or all in one bull-shooting rampage.

Another two-lane gravel road curved off to the south, following an arrow that said EARTHQUAKE FAULTS 16 MILES. They seldom name faults after people. You've got your Pikes Peak but no Pikes Fault, and Mount McKinley but no Fault McKinley. They do have one named after Saint Andreas, but there could be a lot more.

At Eureka, Nevada, the billboard said: WELCOME TO EUREKA—THE LONELIEST TOWN ON THE LONELIEST ROAD IN AMERICA. I could have gone in there to check it out but for some reason I didn't. I drive alone but it doesn't make me lonely, and maybe I didn't want to push my luck. Crossed the broad Reese River Valley, saw eagles and buzzards in the sky and magpies in the ditches, and dust devils off on the flat. Mountains to the east looked like ribbons of suede leather samples, all dusky grays and blues, the tops pure white. I met very few vehicles and don't recall passing any on that marvelous stretch of highway. What a privilege, to drive hour upon hour through a vast and beautiful emptiness.

In Austin, Nevada, in a gas station high in those same mountains, I said to the clerk, "So this is an old Pony Express station," and he said, "Pony Express a hundred years ago—Federal Express today."

A younger man with a hangover brought two big bottles of cold soda to the counter and said, "If I'da known I was gonna be this thirsty today I'da drank more last night."

The first man said, "I heard it was a wild night at the tavern. Wish I'd been there."

"It was a barn burner," the kid said.

East of there in Utah, after a sleep in the truck, I dropped into a vacated land of stone ramparts and canyons beyond description. Driving through at sunrise made me shake my head in disbelief, thinking We don't belong here, it's way too beautiful for the likes of us. Good thing it's empty. US 50 meets Interstate 70 at the town of Salina, in Utah, and for a goodly portion of the freeway the two roadways are separated, giving you the effect of driving on a one-way road through a dreamscape of colored stone.

Stopped at a favorite place in western Colorado, Gay Johnson's Truckstop, tucked up against a high vertical red stone cliff not that far from Grand Junction. There was at one time a small network of these truck stops out there in

the West, and I can't say if they are all still around nowadays or if they have succumbed to the pressure of the big
chains. It'd be a shame.

At the fuel pumps I saw where a semitrailer had been
dragged over a concrete abutment, built to prevent exactly
that from happening. There were fresh gouges from a
driver who turned too sharp pulling away, like I'd done at
the scale at Ray's twenty-two years earlier. I asked the
attendant about it and he said it was kind of a sad deal, a
young guy who had wanted to drive a truck since he was
a kid and then finally got his license and did something
like this in his first week out. "He was pulling a gas tanker
and was lucky there was no fire; the whole damn place
could have gone up. Knocked a pump over and tore the
undercarriage right off the tank. Trailer was a total loss,
and I think maybe it bent the frame on the tractor, too. I
don't think they really wanted to do it, y'know, but they let
him go. Just didn't want to have that accident hanging
over their heads, probably."

"Is this kid a local guy?"

"Yeah. But I think he moved after that. I think he might
have moved to Denver or someplace."

Most drivers like the old smaller fuel stops, and there are
still some fine ones left, like this one. There are also some
real dumps out there. A dump firmly stuck in my head is

an old grimy tile-and-brick monstrosity in Detroit. The floor hadn't felt a mop in weeks. The booths were worn plastic laminate, no upholstery, jagged gashes here and there as if whomped by a sledgehammer. The cashier sat behind bullet-proof glass smeared with some nameless goo. The parking lot was unlit, pitted with potholes like grenade craters. The nearby neighborhood was mostly rubble, looked vaguely like photos of Stalingrad in 1943. I somehow found myself there twice, both times at night and after a rain—I remember the oily black ponds—and the walk in the mud from the cafe to the truck was like a scene from a slasher movie. You could almost hear an ominous soundtrack swelling in the background. A truck here and there had its clearance lights lit, but somehow that made it seem more foreboding. Like silent witnesses. There were cars mixed in back there, never a comforting presence in a truck lot.

The back row where my Kenworth waited seemed a long way into the dark. A silhouette moved silent in the crevasse between nearby trailers. Most likely a driver back there taking a whiz, but I thought at the time I should be carrying something a little more potent than a Leatherman folding tool. A few weeks later, at a produce dock not far from there, a driver who worked for me was held up between trailers at shaky gunpoint by a man so strung out on drugs he could barely talk.

That would take the prize for low-down ominous, but for straight wretched neglect the worst I ever stopped at was a run-down old shambles somewhere in southern Ohio. A place so worn, so bleak, so devoid of human comfort of any sort it made you think of the day room at an old-time poorhouse or a neglected insane asylum, or maybe a bad drunk tank. Despair reeked from every fractured corner and floor-scraping door, from each loose hinge and cracked window. Greenish wallboard lit by bare bulbs curled at the joints; not a single picture hung on any wall, not even a Budweiser poster. Nobody had spent a nickel on the place in decades, the business hanging on until some merciful catastrophe, perhaps a fire or a wayward truck crashing through the pumps, would come along and put it out of its misery. Until then the owner would squeeze every stray dime that might chance by in need of a dirty cup of coffee or some diesel fuel from an oily pump.

None of that by itself was unique in the large world of decaying truck stops. What made this the champ of dozens of contenders, the detail that clinched the title for Buck's Buckeye Truck Stop, was in the men's toilet. Cramped and utterly filthy, it held a single cracked urinal hanging on a yellow-stained wall, and one commode. Inside the beaten doorless stall next to the cracked toilet and its akimbo seat stood the toilet plunger. It was chained to the wall.

Now what kind of clientele would steal a toilet plunger? I couldn't imagine any truck driver, no matter how coarse or rude or crude, bringing something like that back into his own cab. Were they worried about plunger theft by their own employees—had there been a plethora of pilfered plungers?

It later struck me that it may have been chained there as an act of humor. Maybe the whole place exists as that, someone out to prove that no matter how low-down and funky and just plain rotten a business you run, you will still have a market niche.

Arrived in Knoxville well past sunset on Tuesday and found a loading zone for the truck a couple blocks from our hotel. It was a most agreeable downtown, tight side streets canopied with heavy green branches, fine old masonry buildings, long views from the open ends of wider streets. A small park sat in the middle of it all, about the sweetest shadiest little block you could find, cool and dark and floral, overhung with thick greens like a cave. It could have been the backyard of a botanist.

The town was named after Henry Knox, Washington's secretary of war. Like Jesse Reno, he never saw his namesake city. It's been home to a lot of writers, like George Washington Harris, James Agee, the journalist Paul Y. Anderson, and Frances Hodgson Burnett, an English writer of children's stories. And of course Cormac McCarthy, a Tennessee writer of grown-up stories.

There are a lot of others, and there are even more Knoxville musicians, going back to the famous fiddling brothers Bob and Alf Taylor—Bob ended up governor, congressman, and U.S. senator. For quite a while the Sound of Money in Knoxville was the sound of country music, and early rock and roll. The Andrew Johnson Hotel, still standing, held a radio station on its top floor and sent out the music of Chet Atkins, Roy Acuff, Homer and Jethro, Kitty Wells, the Carter Sisters, the Everly Brothers, Archie Campbell, Pee Wee King, and hundreds more. Rock and roll saw early beginnings here in the persons of Brownie and Stick McGhee. Hank Williams was last seen alive in the Andrew Johnson on New Year's Eve of 1952; was helped into the backseat of that Cadillac by porters, on his way to Ohio. The driver stopped in West Virginia, where they found that Hank had gone on ahead.

Saturday night we loaded out of the Civic Center, across the river from downtown, and as much as I wanted to spend another night there I was even more anxious to get home. Took off and put on some hundreds of miles I don't remember, slept in the truck, and got back late Sunday. It was a day or two before I realized what a great spring it had been. Peoria, Butte, Greeley, Reno, Knoxville—old-time rough and rowdy places built with whiskey, beer, and bulldozers; gold, silver and copper; religion, temperance, farmland, and cattle; railroads, gambling, marriage, and divorce—and polishing it off in a hometown for southern literature, country music, and rock and roll. The end of another season, and I don't expect it's going to get much better than all that.

7

TOMATOES, LOVE LETTERS, AND TURKEYS

IT WAS WET IN THE SPRING OF 1999, AND tomatoes in low ground were not doing that great. The subject came up at an afternoon music venue—a bar with a band outside—when a friend introduced me to this hefty biker, a machinist by trade, who raised tomatoes and built custom motorcycles. He also knew the guys at a scrap metal yard and had access to junk. The big fella said that weighing over three hundred pounds made it miserable for him to get down there on his knees and weed and all that business, and he had figured out a way to avoid that. He said we'd be impressed. We were riding north from St. Paul anyway so we stopped at his house to see his Harleys and his tomato garden.

We arrived to a long driveway lined with young trees. He had an electric door opener on an unpainted old split-board shed. He punched the remote with a flourish and the old door rose and there sat two striking custom bikes, all gleaming chrome and bright iridescent paint in an otherwise colorless garage. They jumped out at you. One was five deep shades of blue and the other was red and orange. They were set low to the ground like custom bikes are and they both had fat rear tires but the orange-and-red one had a skinny front tire and extended forks while the blue had a heavier look, with big front forks and a fat tire up there as well—not as fat as the rear one, but fat. There was a working lift he could raise them on. We admired his welding and the various tasteful details around the rear axles, the mounting of the exhaust pipes, the custom air cleaners he had designed and fabricated. The hand-stitched leather seats. The guy was an artist. A big rough-looking artist, and heavy into finesse.

He took us out back to the garden. Twenty-four green fifty-five-gallon drums were arranged in four perfect rows on dead-level short grass, walled to the north by a tight line of tall straight American cedar trees and surrounded on the east and west by solid hedges. It looked like it had a purpose, something beyond the idea of inexpensive tomatoes. Something connected to the universe, or a secret society. The tomato plants were up and full and looking lush, already reaching over the rims of the barrels.

He said a few years back he was at the junkyard and saw four fifty-five-gallon steel drums, and a tiny little light went on in his tiny little brain. He brought them home and set them behind the garage, filled them with dirt, and put a Big Boy in each one and they did well. Next year he got four more drums. He now had the precise twenty-four-drum formation, squat formal columns holding well-tended plants in a very green stand-up garden. He said he liked that number, twenty-four. It was agreeable. You could divide it by 2, 3, 4, 6, 8, and 12, and it had other properties as well, which he didn't go into. The fruits would be Earlys, Romanos, little salad ones, big ones, all orange and green and red. He said by late summer they'd spread a waist-high green plain out there, like a pond.

"No bending, no hoeing. Keeps the critters out, too," he said. "I'm a pioneer. The fat pioneer of tomato farming. Hahahaha! I got some fat tomatoes, too!"

I said I was surprised at how formal it was. "I know," he said. "Looks like some kinda ancient mystery or somethin'. I didn't have that in mind, but when I set 'em out there, y'know, I kinda had to line 'em up in straight rows, like I couldn't help myself. And I really don't need twenty-four tomato plants—I mean I can't give away even half the tomatoes I get. But once I got started I just kinda went with it. It was sort of an accident that it ended up like this. And these trees were already here when I bought the place, and they kinda added to it. I like it, though; I like to stand out here and work on 'em. It's kinda cosmic."

When we left he said, "Come on by in about six weeks and bring some bags. I'll give ya all the tomatoes you can carry. Any color, any kind."

When I first saw this huge guy standing at the bar, with that big gut and the tattoos and the old leather vest and the big beard and that don't-gimme-no-crap look, about the last thing I would have connected him to would have been a formal garden.

We took another motorcycle ride out west that summer, three of us. It's different from traveling by truck. We take two-lane roads and stop every 120 miles or so, talk to people, look around the mountains, ride the canyons along whitewater rivers. Sometimes take pictures. From a truck you're an overhead observer, at least until you find enough acreage to park it, and then you're a pedestrian. Usually a kind of stiff-legged, slow-moving one.

On the bike you get punished a little for your intrusion, especially without a windshield. If it rains you get soaked clean through, even in leathers, and you ride for a couple of hours when you get out of it, at least if it's a morning rain, and your machine becomes an eighteen-thousand-dollar clothes dryer. You get windburned and covered with gnats and bees and dust and that all makes the stops even better. The locals don't say it but they appreciate the fact that you suffer a little to come out and see what they get for free every day.

The biggest difference is that on the bike you can go in the bars, and out west is where they have the best ones. They stand as museums to the independent past, some layered in photographs, some with dollar bills hanging from the ceiling, some slathered with rude signs and license plates, one bristling with half-dollars and quarters driven into the log roof beams with an old hammer borrowed from the bar; some with live music, some with loud jukeboxes, some with scarred floors, old bullet wounds, animal heads with glass eyes, stuffed jackrabbits with horns, granddaddy shotguns with cracked wood stocks hung up out of reach, photographs of herds and mountains, fancy mirrors. There is also a lot of fine woodwork in the background out there, speaking of an elegance no longer on the market.

The Friday after we got back, the last Friday of July, I was at Neumann's in North St. Paul, waiting for my old band Scooter Trash to set up and play, and I ran into Armand, a guy I used to work with back when I wore a jacket and tie to work. He's now in his middle years, I'd guess maybe early to midfifties, and we took a far table and did a little catching up on things. And on people we'd worked for and with.

And then he told me that he was cleaning his own little corner of their attic just this last June, a job he'd been putting off almost from the day he and his wife moved into that house in 1988, and he found an old cardboard box that had once held a tape deck. It was the last one, late in the day, the bottom box of the stack on the inside row against the corner. It was marked MISC OFFICE in felt pen and was held together with dried and brittle masking tape. He wasn't sure what might be in there.

He found it held old letters from a woman. From Carolyn, his first love. There were a lot of them. They had written to each other two and three times a week over three years when they were in college; the box had been through two moves and somehow never been opened. He read the first one on the pile, which was one of the last ones she wrote, not a hint of the impending breakup. She was newsy, affectionate, funny, and she missed him. She was looking forward to seeing him. He said he got all tingly reading it. It had been a while since a woman had found him interesting enough to look forward to seeing him. At least to just come right out and say it like that.

She wrote them from Carleton College; he was in St. Cloud at the time, later to transfer to the university in Minneapolis. It had been nearly thirty years. He read another and it gave him such a rush of youth and outright happiness that it brought him nearly to tears. It probably did bring him to tears and he didn't want to say that.

Anyway, he moved the box of letters to a high shelf in the garage among boxes of wire and old fishing tackle and discarded auto parts, on top of which lay a folded tarp. When he left for work in the morning he took one letter with him in the inside pocket of his coat and hoped he didn't have a heart attack that day and they'd find it on him.

It became his pattern, to read one letter a day, to have his spirits lifted, to recall her smile and her touch. He knew she'd married some guy who had been doing well in the corporate world, 3M or General Mills or something like that, but he hadn't heard news of her in years. The present Carolyn wasn't the Carolyn in the letters anyway, he knew that, just as he wasn't the same wild happy kid she was writing to.

But it was a resurrection, to be raised again into the free and optimistic youth he'd been: the flat belly, the long hair, the adrenaline running, the wonder of the immense world out there and him not quite realizing he had the keys to it. He marveled at the letters, the flow of her pen, the simple words, the directness, the complete unabashed honesty of the whole thing. They were on a good stationery and unfolded easily. He was glad that corner of the attic didn't leak and that no squirrels had ever gotten in there.

For a month he read a letter every day, metering them out. A chemistry test coming up, a story she'd read, something a guy had said in class, some instructor that was a cut above; dinner with friends. Things they had done together the previous weekend. She spoke to him of entire days long forgotten, bringing back scenes and sounds and the very smell of being young; a date they had in a Corvette borrowed from a friend; a strange country band in a small-town bar where they drank pitcher after pitcher of beer with two local couples; a crazy hockey game. A time at a resort in Wisconsin when he had thrown her off a pier fully clothed and then jumped in after her. The time they went skiing and he punched a rich creep at the lodge who'd spilled a drink on her and laughed about it.

Sometimes the letters would nearly overpower him. "Why can't we, just once each year, go back to some one day of long ago? What a gift that would be," he said, and here she was giving him exactly that. And she didn't even know about it. He wondered what she was doing right now, just as he used to wonder that exact same thing the first time he read these letters. He would think: What is she doing right now? He would picture her perfect face . . . at the time he thought it would drive him crazy.

But then he wondered, What *is* she doing? He thought of finding out where she was. He'd like to tell her about the old letters and how sweet they were and how great they were to find. They had a few mutual friends in the city. She wouldn't be hard to find. He could make inquiries, maybe even on the Internet. It would be harmless, but it wasn't something he'd want his wife to find out about. So maybe he shouldn't. But what the hell.

What if he found her and she wanted to go to lunch, he thought; would he do it? Would one thing lead to another? Maybe she's lonely, maybe her husband doesn't interest her anymore, either, like he doesn't seem to interest his own wife. A guy could end up in big trouble. This is really playing with dynamite, isn't it? This is stupid. But what the hell.

It took only three phone calls to friends to find her phone number and address. They said she was living near Lake Harriet in south Minneapolis, had divorced and remarried. Been there since 1992 or so.

He said that a few days later on his lunch break he drove by her place, a fine old redbrick house, big trees, a shady mysterious backyard, a trellis, a garage that had once been a carriage house; he saw the steep slate roof and the dormers and the cupola with the weather vane on top and knew that it was far more elegant than anything he would ever own.

That weekend when his wife was out shopping, Armand said, he took the letters, of which he had by then increased his pace and read about half, and kept out one of his favorites and put the rest in a plastic bag and drove his old Jeep to a Dumpster behind a strip mall near his house and threw them over the lip. The one he saved was not the most passionate nor the one in which he was most admired or the most heroic; but it had something in it that revealed a genuine lonesomeness, a longing she had at the time, to be with him. She had missed him then like he thought he missed her now. When he got home he sat in the Jeep for a long time before he went into the house.

He never called Carolyn and he doesn't drive by her house and he thinks maybe he's pretty sure he's not jealous of her husband. Or of her either, for the grand life she must be leading.

But just that week he told me all this, that previous Tuesday morning, he had put the one letter he had been saving in a brown paper grocery bag with a bunch of other papers and set them out at the curb for recycling. He didn't leave for work until he saw the truck come by and stop and the young man hop out and throw the bag in the big wire-mesh bin and haul it away. He thought the kid was about the same age he had been when he got the letter.

The band started and sounded terrific and made me wish I was still with them, doing those raucous blues and that early Chuck-Berry-style rock and roll. Armand stayed for the first set and said he had to leave. Keep in touch, we both said. I stayed there until the place closed.

•••

My motorcycle pal Jim told me a story about his ex-brother-in-law named Frank Garrett, who had the past spring caught a tom turkey by hand. Tom turkeys are among the world's most cautious creatures, hard to hunt even with a shotgun. It's a real trick to get within fifty feet of one under any circumstances. Frank is a big guy, half Sioux, with a place up west and north of the town, an old farmstead with a few head of cattle and two dogs, and he leads, as much by default as by design, a quasi-natural existence; drives a school bus and does repair work for people and gets by with a garden and some geese. He's lived by himself ever since his second wife left him on New Year's Eve of 1995.

He was driving on a gravel road near his place when he saw economic opportunity in the personage of a good-sized wild turkey hen walking along the edge of a field of corn stubble. He slowed and saw her slip into the woods. He followed on foot; she was sitting on a nest and flew when he approached. There were five eggs. He figured she probably couldn't count anyway and he could take three of them and start his own flock.

Back at the pickup he eased the eggs into an old rag of a bath towel and drove gingerly home, folding the cloth so as to keep them separated. He put the eggs on the towel in a wooden crate under a forty-watt bulb in the garage. He liked the idea so much he took a cloth bag and went back the next day for the other two, thinking that just the three wouldn't be enough for a good start and the hen could always have another brood anyway. Give her a reason to go back into heat; do her a favor. She was on the nest when he got there and she rose in alarm, yelping, a great flapping of wings, cries of outrage as she flew off into a tree. He reached in for the eggs, and was startled by a piercing gobble from directly behind, a shriek of pure uncontrolled animal rage, and he turned to the amazing sight of a puffed-out tom turkey in full charge. Coming at him like a freight train.

The distance between them disappeared in a second. He was still in shock when the bird hit him, spurs up, spurs sharp as thorns and long as bear claws, and going for a stranglehold got him a couple of quick slices on his thighs. He was hollering cusswords and the turkey was gobbling and shrieking; he went for the bird's feet and quickly found himself on the ground holding its left leg above the spur, and being ripped across the midsection by the right. He was speared twice in the palm reaching for the free leg before he got a good grip on it. He rolled over and picked himself up, holding the bird upside down by both feet, and found some twine in the bed of the pickup. He tied the feet together and took off his denim jacket, wrapped it around the bird, tied the sleeves together, and hoisted it over the side. He took the bag back to the nest to get the eggs. He was bleeding from four or five places and thinking he might end up killing this stinking bird if it didn't get him first. And what a shock; nothing in his hunting experience had ever indicated that tom turkeys were family men.

He cushioned the bag of eggs in a tire with some gunnysacks and figured if he left the tom back in the bed with them it'd struggle loose for sure and fly off, so he brought it inside the cab. On the way back to the farm he drove with his left hand and tried to keep the bird under control with his right, but the twine at the ankles came loose and it started kicking and ripping the jacket with big tearing sounds until it kicked free of the sleeves and set to flapping and crapping at the same time, disgusting white and black and greenish liquid spraying around the cab, but still it was the least of his worries at the time because the tom came at him again and again, filling Frank's entire world with feathers, flashing spurs, and blind fury. He felt a knife cut a long slice from his right jaw to the hairline at the temple. He had the choice of rolling the truck or being shredded at the wheel, or, he thought, maybe both.

He made a quick and lucky one-handed move and this time caught the bird by the neck, banging it hard back into the seat, again and again, shouting, "Settle down and stop kicking you son of a bitch or I'll kill you right here do you hear me?" and after some time the wattle began to turn white from the stranglehold. The bird quieted to almost limp as he came to his driveway but when he released it to make the turn in two heartbeats the tom came roaring back to life, spurs and beak and shitter and wings all going at once again. Frank hit the brakes, shifted into park, and bailed out the driver's door; the turkey leaped over and flapped its way past the steering wheel after him and Frank grabbed a leg and they ended up on the ground in the yard like a tussle on Main Street in a western movie and he got gashed again, on the stomach and shoulder, but was able to grab the tom's neck high underneath the beak and he brought the head down and pinned it against its left leg with one hand. It was a real barnyard ruckus, his geese honking and then the dogs closing in, barking up a frenzy, spittle flying. He swore a streak and wrapped the ripped jacket around the black feathers and said, "You goddamn, worthless pile of chickenshit-bullshit-dogshit-sonofabitch-go-to-hell-god*DAMN* bastard, stinking-ass rotten miserable, ugly, jackass . . . TURKEYBIRD," the worst thing he could think of, and he threw the bird in the shed and slammed the door and latched it.

He put the two new eggs under the low heat with their siblings and went in the house to clean up. In the mirror he looked like he'd been in a knife fight with a whole gang, blood all over his hands and face and chest and belly. The slices on the face and belly were in there a ways but not deep enough to make him go to town for stitches—not that he would under any circumstance—so he laid disinfectant on heavy and set Band-Aids across them like bridges; the rest were more or less routine farmer-carpenter type hand and forearm cuts. He went out to the pickup and found it pasted inside with feathers and great dramatic swatches and streaks of black-and-white turkey hurlings and it stunk and he could see little splatters of blood mixed in, his own blood, and he had to suppress an urge to put on leather gloves and go back out to the shed and kill that bird once and for all, the two of them, fight to the death and be done with it.

Jim went up to see him that same fall. They were going to leave from Frank's place in Jim's four-by-four and drive out to South Dakota to hunt turkeys, an expedition they usually mount on even-numbered years to escape election news. Jim was surprised to see the flock of wild turkeys in the big high chicken-wire enclosure. Frank told him the whole story with all the details and showed him the shed where he kept the tom; when he opened the door the bird instantly flew up and charged them, spurs up. He shut the door and said, "That turkey hates my guts."

"I got that impression," said Jim.

Frank said, "You know me. I've been married and divorced twice and a lot of other crazy stuff, been mean to people, fought guys, did stuff I shouldn't have. But I have never had anybody hate me like that turkey does. He is pure raw hatred. He thinks he's gonna kill me every day; it's probably the only thing he ever thinks about. I bring him food and water and he'd still rather kill me than anything in the world. He'd be happy to starve to death just to kill me. I hated him right back, too, at first, but after a couple of weeks my hand quit hurting and I sort of got over it. I can't say I much care for him, but it's not like it was. I let him in with his little family now and then, but it doesn't do any good. He's just mean, through and through. Mean and angry and full of hate, and dumb as a stick."

Jim said, "Y'know Frank, it seems a little funny to drive six hundred miles out to South Dakota to shoot turkeys when we could just shoot this one right here. This one's probably bigger than anything we're gonna see out there anyway."

Frank looked at him. "I know we could. But living here by myself . . . I have to say . . . I guess it's okay to have something around that hates your guts. It's healthy, 'cause at least I've got one creature around here who isn't trying to get on my good side. The dogs, they schmooze hell out of a person, and the cattle and the rest are always glad to see you; they see me and they see food. But this bird, y'know, he brings real honest feelings to the place. He lets me know what he thinks of me. A guy's got to respect that."

"Hell. You wouldn't miss him. I bet you'd be glad to get rid of the hassle."

"Ya, but it's not just that, either. I couldn't shoot this bird because it wouldn't be right. I mean, y'know, we fight hand and claw. If he was anything but a turkey one of us might be dead by now—if he was a chicken I'd have killed him a long time ago, and if he was a bull or something, he'd've killed me. So I'd feel sneaky if I just up and shot him . . . it'd be like shooting your sparring partner. Y'know, it's different out there in the wild, tracking some big old turkey you don't even know. But I know this guy. If I shot him I'd feel like I broke the rules. Besides, I don't go out hunting for the shooting anyway, not really. That's just icing on the cake, getting a bird. I just like to get away. You know how that is, right?"

8
CRAZY HORSE AND MILLENNIUM FEVER

A WARM FALL CAME ON. THEY WERE brutal, those nice days. The fantastic colors all around made it all the worse, leaves showing us how to die: Go out with a big show, full of sugar, like dying at a great banquet, full of desserts and the best wines, dressed your finest, never looked better; and all your friends are there and they look fabulous and they all die, too. How magnificent.

It slipped into October and the 1999 fall season had started and the show was up and running at the Fitzgerald. As of the morning of the fifteenth, the threatening chill had left and we were enjoying the second warm autumn in a row. Along the creekbeds and in the sharp valleys aspens, birches, and maples were hanging on to some last leaf or two, bright flecks against the oaks' ruddy maroons. Cut rows of brittle corn stubble curved up and around the hills like rough fabric. Round hay bales settled near barns and along fence lines as if they had rolled in on their own, and in some yards great sheets of plastic restrained piles of grain, weighted against the wind with tires and concrete blocks.

There was a purpose on the countryside, in fields neatly cut, machinery set in straight lines, yards cleaned, nothing lying at random. Like the buttoned-down deck of a massive ship, prepared to take on storms with sheer stubborn neatness. The next night we dropped out of the fifties and forties and into the twenties; frost warnings were out for Sunday night, twenty-eight degrees, possible snow on Tuesday. Here at last was winter. Bring it on, we said.

But it still didn't get all that cold. In November we were heading to New York for another holiday stand at the Town Hall, but this year instead of the shortcut through Atlanta we went by way of Rapid City, South Dakota. On the way into the city I floated over a soft landscape of light brown suede etched with that fine grid that lies over the prairies, a few square patches of faded dark green, all very smooth until the approach to the valley of the Cheyenne River, where it began to break into dark jagged canyons and the rectangular pattern gave up at the edges of low hills to faint curving trails, like scrollwork on the slopes. The freeway crossed the river directly below where the airliners cross it; struck me odd that they'd use the same place to cross a river. I slipped in over a rise in the grassland prairie and saw the craggy mountain skyline off to the west.

The drive into the city passed through the usual light industry, past a little green sign that said RAPID CITY POPU-LATION 54,523 and the billboard that said REPTILE GAR-DENS—LAST CHANCE THIS CENTURY TO GET YOUR SEASON'S PASS, and at the core there sat a typical western town: finely detailed brick and stone three-story buildings and the railroad tracks running parallel with the main drag just like they're supposed to. The streets were wide enough to park diagonally and still have three lanes in the middle so people could back out into traffic. A sign on the side of a corner store read: BUFFALO SKULLS AND ROBES—BEADWORK—JEWELRY—THE WORLD'S LARGEST SELECTION OF ITALIAN GLASS BEADS.

I arrived to barricades and the echoing sound of bands playing. A Veterans Day parade moved down St. Joseph Street, sounding bigger than it was. They don't make much of this holiday where I live, an area of delicate sensibilities where they turn away from the suggestion of necessary violence. Out in the realistic West they have no problem with stopping traffic for a celebration of geezers who went through hell and actually had to kill people. Spectators called out to white-haired guys in the backs of pickup trucks and they waved back; an unadorned five-year-old Chevy pickup truck carried seven old guys sitting on hay bales and they got a big hand, as if they were movie stars.

After the bands and the Legion and the VFW and the

DAV and the Knights of Columbus and the Shriners and the Boy Scouts came the ROTC color guard with the flags and the spinning rifles with an officer of the guard in a chrome helmet marching alongside. And after that rolled the National Guard, kids in fatigues driving HUMVEEs and six-by-six trucks, and the grand finale, a World War II half-track—half truck and half tank. Hadn't seen one in thirty years. I recalled a World War II veteran saying, "The problem with the half-track was that it was like me—too light for heavy work and too heavy for light work." I figured they must have been about right for medium work.

Had lunch downtown, left the trailer at the hotel parking lot and headed north on I-90 to take a circle tour of the Black Hills. Passed the sign that says WONDERLAND CAVE— AS TOLD BY NEW YORK TIMES—BRING YOUR CAMERA and the one that says OLD FORT MEADE CAVALRY MUSEUM, and turned at the Sturgis exit by the Hog Heaven RV Park: CABINS—CAMPING—RESORT. Sturgis is also home to the National Motorcycle Museum but I didn't stop in.

I did tour Dakota Arms, a shop where they build some of the world's most elegant rifles, one at a time. The rifle bolts are milled of oil-glistening steel and hand-fitted into a most satisfying motion, slick and smooth and solid enough to feel like the lock on a bank vault. I wondered what I might sell to have an exquisite work of art like this.

I'm too lazy to hunt so I'd just have it around and talk about hunting. Do a little target practice; show it off and get a reputation as a gun nut. Which might be useful.

The sun came low through the birch-and-cedar forest and made black streaks across the road. The old towns of Deadwood, Lead, and Hill City fell behind and the truck seemed to be floating through paradise. High meadows gave glimpses through distant passes to lands beyond, of dark and quiet lakes. It made a person feel he had no business there. I arrived at a blinking yellow light on the highway and a small sign, took a left into the drive, and there it was, still two miles off but clear and unmistakable: the mountain cut into the face of Crazy Horse, just like in the pictures. Breathtaking.

In the shop there I learned it is the largest sculptural undertaking in the history of the world, eighty feet higher than the Pyramid of Giza, eight feet taller than the Washington Monument; the face alone is more than eighty-seven feet high, seventeen feet taller than the Sphinx. All four Rushmore faces would fit inside the head.

The sculptor was Korczak Ziolkowski, who died in 1982 at the age of seventy-four and who worked on the project continuously from 1947 until his death, taking time off now and then to deal with, in chronological order over thirty-four years, a back injury from a broken cable, a broken wrist and thumb, a back operation to remove two lower discs, another back operation to remove the third disc, a third operation to remove the fourth and fifth discs, a heart attack, a more massive heart attack, worsening diabetes and arthritis, a separated Achilles tendon, an operation to remove the sixth disc, and, just before his death, a quadruple bypass operation. And over this time he and his wife Ruth raised ten children.

He had been invited to carve the memorial by Sioux chiefs after he won first place at the New York World's Fair in 1939 for a marble portrait called *Paderewski: Study of an Immortal.* He never took a nickel from the government, twice turning down ten-million-dollar federal grant offers; he was determined to keep the government out of it, that it be financed only by interested parties, and he never took a salary.

His wife and children have carried on the work. In 1991 the profile emerged against the sky for the first time. Now the left arm of Crazy Horse stretches out before him. The forefinger will someday point, capturing a moment when a white man had asked the taunting question, "Where are your lands now?" and he had replied, "My lands are where my dead lie buried."

A dramatic poem by the sculptor will be carved in the stone behind Crazy Horse, in letters three feet high on a giant tablet. It's a moving place. Hard to describe and hard to resist. So I reacted as my years of training had taught me: I bought some Indian silver in the gift shop. I was the only customer in there. The sun had just set and only the chief's profile stood brightly lit above the green of the mountains; I watched it in the rearview mirror all the way back to the main road.

It occurred to me that in the reach of history this will stand as the Sphinx or as Machu Picchu stands, as much a mysterious remnant of a lost civilization as the message to the descendants it was intended to be. And even that might not matter as much as the simple physical fact that it will be there at all, the mightiest project ever undertaken by one single human in all of history.

Leaving there and heading for Rapid City I came around behind the Mount Rushmore faces in the dark. The street lights were on and the empty tollbooth was lit in a green light. The gates were raised.

The presidents looked out exactly as expected, except the uplight from footlights below made them seem like seated actors downstage at the opening of a play, looking out seriously over a hushed audience of concrete parking ramps. They looked like they'd never expected to end up like this, playing to an empty house.

I drove through vertical-wall canyons like New York, like Fifth Avenue on a moonless night in a power failure. The spell broke at the town of Keystone, all brightly lit,

with another of those Main Streets that have been completely repainted and restored to a condition that shows
the easterner what a boardwalk wood-frame town in the
Old West would have looked like if it had been painted
bright colors all at once and had a clean four-lane concrete main drag, instead of all the unpainted wood and
mud and horse manure that it did have.

As I came in on US 16 from the west, Rapid City lay
below like a great bed of glowing coals, mixed pale blues
and orange embers, spread all through the valley like
glimmerings of a fading campfire in a shallow swale.

A hanging tree still stands high on Skyline Drive, a tall
desolate dead trunk with only the stubs of branches left. I
read that in 1877 a posse overtook a pair of thieves named
Red Curry and Doc Allen, catching them red-handed with
six stolen horses. There was a third man with them, a fellow named Hall who just happened to be riding along that
day. They were taken to a cabin that served as the Pen-
nington County Jail. A midnight mob came and took them
from prison and hung Red and Doc—and even knowing
that Hall had stolen no horses, he swore so much they figured he must be guilty of something so they strung him up
as well. It was a badly bungled execution. The branch they
were hung from was too low to use a horse for the gallows
trapdoor so the posse substituted rocks, which they
kicked out from under the feet of the unlucky three. The

posse rode off and the branch bent down from the weight and their struggling toeprints were scratched into the ground as they choked to death. For years folks from nearby towns referred to the residents of Rapid City as "Stranglers."

I left there Sunday morning and got home for a short break before heading to New York, where we would settle in for another year-end stand. Only this time it would be an end-of-the-'90s stand, plus an end-of-the-century stand, and on top of that an end-of-the-millennium stand.

• • •

The first snowfall that Tuesday, the sixteenth of November, 1999, came on very light at first, highlighting and engraving each blade and leaf in the backyard, a beautiful black-and-white etching that resembled photos taken with electron microscopes, the incredible fine powdery detail they give. It could have been the crystalline structure of a metallic surface, like the blade of a knife magnified a thousand times, or the armored shell of a beetle.

It didn't linger in the fine-etching mode for long. It soon fell in heavy wet flakes, like the kisses of an overenthused girl after too many beers. Flakes that when they hit your pant leg you felt a wet cold spot right away. Two to four inches possible by nightfall, they said, and I expected a slippery highway next morning.

But it let up before noon. Turned out to be the seasonal equivalent of a head fake, just a quick little reminder that there are other seasons lurking around here. I left on Wednesday and by the time I reached mid-Wisconsin it was gone without a trace. I had begun using I–94 by Milwaukee and into Chicago instead of the shorter I–90, to avoid the massive clotting at the five cursed tollbooths on the way in. The trip to New York was routine with good weather all the way. I got there Thursday, parked the rig on Eleventh Avenue and had barbecue dinner with the crew at Virgil's, the famous place on 44th. There was work to be done in the morning so we didn't stop at Jimmy's Corner.

Friday morning I brought the truck to the front of the theater and caught up on the logbook while the crew unloaded. The trailer lurched heavily as they moved the big steel road closets back and down the aluminum ramp. The Kit Kat Club sat across the street in the old Henry Miller's Theatre; that night stretch limos were pulling up there like pickup trucks at a Clint Black concert. The marquee read: IN HERE LIFE IS BEAUTIFUL.

I left the equipment there for the next four weeks and drove back. The trip home was as routine as the trip out, and two weeks later on a Wednesday morning, the fourteenth of December, it was snowing lightly but with vigor;

the flakes were small, nearly invisible, but they were coming in on a hard wind and in certain places, like on the driveway and under the bird feeders, they'd gathered together into visible white settlements. There was now a chance of having snow on the ground for Christmas, not a big deal in most of the United States but it is here, where people don't feel like it's a real Christmas without snow in the yard. That wind was a honed knife cutting through the jacket, making snowdrift enthusiasts optimistic.

The next Sunday morning there came a soft warm snowfall, continuing on through the day, building to three inches and still coming down. A muffling layer that held the promise of being with us for a while; they said the temperatures would be below freezing for the rest of the week, and there was a possibility for snow the next day as well. That night the moon imprinted the trees so brightly on the snow that from the upstairs windows the yard looked like a woodcut.

Monday brought a clear sky and a beautiful warm-looking orange sunrise, and in less than an hour fine icy flakes were whipping by the door. By afternoon the windchill was forty below zero, a murdering wind under a bright sun. I went out to fill the bird feeders and the wind sliced right through to the nerve endings, drilled right in until it hit bone. I couldn't blame nature for trying to murder me but I wished she wasn't in such a hurry.

The snow stayed and we had our ivory Christmas, although I spent it on the road. Our last show of the twentieth century was on the evening of Christmas Day, which meant driving to New York on the twenty-third and twenty-fourth and back to St. Paul on the twenty-sixth and twenty-seventh.

It seemed strange that we were all so calm about this end of the second millennium. It was a big deal to me to reach the end of a century, much less the end of a thousand years. There was an avalanche of quickie books out there of course and a great deal of Internet blather, but there were no parades or streets filled with people dancing and drinking and making a ruckus about it. It was an amazing privilege; what percent of all people who have ever lived have been around at the change of a millennium? I would bet less than a hundredth of a percent, up to now. It's only happened once before. I tried to find out what folks were up to on December 31, A.D. 999, and it seems there was a good deal of apocalyptic fear and a lot of church construction in the years surrounding that date, but no documentation at all of any single huge celebration. From what I read, they were more scared than pleased about the whole thing. It was pretty much the same this time around. (I incidentally learned that Cordova, Spain, was the world's largest city at the time, with about 450,000 inhabitants.)

I used to think about the turning of 2000 when I was a little kid, ten years old, wondering if I would last that long and if I did what it would be like. (It was a small town, not that much to think about there, so I thought about that; once in while, at least, before I started to think about girls.) Pictured gigantic bonfires and bands and fireworks, and roaring crowds as far as the eye could see. I imagined this would take place outdoors in some vast valley, an immense secular celebration; I didn't see any preachers or popes there, or any authority figures at all. There were just common folk in the crowd, as best as I remember the fantasy, and nobody at all in suits.

At sixteen we were drinking beer and anything else that would do the job and we were driving old cars, not poor me but those of us who had cars, and when Chuck's old Pontiac reached 99,900 we got an illegal case of beer and laid it by. When it hit 99,985 four of us went for a ride in the country on a Saturday afternoon and when the odometer rolled on its back to show 00,000.0 we pulled into a field road and had a party. Odometers didn't go to six figures in those days.

At twenty-two, when my 1941 Plymouth four-door sedan with the exhaust pipe bent out in front of the rear wheel—the cheapest thing I could do to make it cool—turned itself back to its prenatal factory mileage I took my college roommates out in the country north of Fargo for a similar late-afternoon celebration. We thought it was an event worth noting.

But when the year 2000—an event of even greater magnitude than my odometer changing—came close upon us nothing seemed to be different at all. People I talked to, nobody even mentioned it. Asked some friends what was happening on New Year's Eve and nobody I knew was even having a party. I was the only one who thought it was a big deal, and I was determined to at least go out and hear some live music in a crowd of happy strangers. I would take them in whatever states of consciousness and coherence they happened to be, and they'd all be my goofy new twenty-first-century pals.

The turning of the year, especially that year, had brought the usual volley of predictions, advice, resolution, and reflection, the stuff of fortune cookies, and I wondered, Where is the mass hedonism in these last weeks of this amazing thousand years? Is it only in Minnesota that we are so blasé about all of this? People fill the streets for two days following a World Series victory; Mardi Gras and spring break and the Sturgis Rally draw hundreds of thousands, for no good reason other than to have a good time. Saint Patrick's Day gets more attention than this. Can it be that one night in Times Square on television will satisfy the need to celebrate the great turning of the millennium for the entire country?

I sat in a cafe in a small town all the way through lunch and they talked about things like dogs. An old man said, They want to give me a dog but I don't want no damn dog, he'll just run out in the street and get run over. And they talked about all the houses being built out there at the edge of town and the roads all being widened and new traffic lights coming in and what a pain in the ass that all was, and about the Vikings losing two cliffhangers in a row and how things were not looking that good anymore for a playoff spot. I sat through all this variety of conversation and never heard a single word about the upcoming end of the second millennium, the most remarkable thousand years in the planet's four-billion-year history.

The computer was the cause of the indifference, of course, with all the Y2K disasters hanging over everyone's head. People were tired of all the yammering about it. Tired of the fearmongering and the agitation. Most people I asked said they'd just stay home on New Year's. Someone of importance should have been saying it was a big deal, worthy of celebration, but no one did. When I was ten and imagining the moment, I never factored in the computer, and of course couldn't have predicted how it would ruin the Big Day.

9

A BOOKKEEPER'S BATTLE WITH FICTION

WITH SIX WEEKS AT HOME IN THE Fitzgerald Theater in St. Paul there was time to catch up with other business. I spent a snow day cleaning up my desk and its surrounding mess and found this little nugget from 150 years earlier, a simpler and sterner time, the April 1849 issue of *Scientific American*. I don't have *Scientific American*s lying around the house that are 150 years old. This came from a flashback in the April '99 issue:

From the Mount Hope Institute of the Insane, Dr. W. H. Stokes says, in respect to moral insanity:

Another fertile source of this species of derangement appears to be an undue indulgence in the perusal of the numerous works of fiction, with which the press is so prolific of late years, and which are sown widely over the land, with the effect of vitiating the taste and corrupting the morals of the young. Parents cannot too cautiously guard their young daughters against this pernicious practice.

It would be this humble typist's faint fondest hope: that he might someday write a work of fiction so vile, so powerful, and so vitiating of taste as to corrupt the morals of someone's daughter. Not yours or mine, of course, but someone's; some daughter under a too-repressive parental guard. Do her a favor and free her from tyrannical caution and autocratic good taste.

Fiction was at its zenith in the nineteenth century; it was to them what rock and roll was to the next century. A pernicious practice. And *vitiate* is such an excellent word. My fat Random House dictionary says: "To impair the quality of; make faulty; spoil, mar. To debase; corrupt; pervert. To make legally defective or invalid, as: to vitiate a claim. Derived from the latin *vitiare*, to spoil." A southern writer could have someone say: "LeRoy Bob, you are behavin' in a most pernicious mannah, and if you do not desist forthwith I shall find myself compelled to vitiate yore haid with this heah hammuh."

Midwesterners never talked that mixture of directness and elegance, but it seems natural coming from southerners—at least as portrayed by southern writers.

And how about the Mount Hope Institute of the Insane? Notice it wasn't *for* but *of*, as if it was the staff and faculty who were insane. And *insane* itself is another excellent word they are trying to strike from our lexicon, although they still allow us *insanity plea* and *sane*. The insane bastards. Rise against them, I say. Stand firm, all ye lovers of direct and straightforward language.

Glenda Waters is a married lady in a small Minnesota town who has worked thirty years as a bookkeeper in a feed mill. She retired not long ago and people asked what she'd do with the rest of her life. They asked if she was going to get even more serious about gardening, or if she thought she'd travel or just spend more time babysitting the grandkids, and she'd say that she'd be happy to sleep late and not work and beyond that she hadn't really thought too much about it. But in fact she had thought quite a bit about it and she knew exactly what she wanted to do.

Her job had been mostly numbers. Her husband was a wonderful man but a farmer of the pre-baby-boom generation and therefore of the old taciturn school of interpersonal relationships. Didn't say much. Most of her conversations were a quick good morning to the boss, explanations to mill hands and farmers about the pay-check, and exchanges with auditors and managers of ag businesses. Not many conversations that weren't about numbers.

So retirement for Glenda was going to be a goodbye to the numeric world and hello to the language of love and that language would be English and she would write a romance novel. She had borrowed a few from the library and figured it had to be easier than accounting.

She told only her husband and two closest friends, Eva and Robert, the neighbors. They were supportive but skeptical, thinking it too ambitious a project, and it was known that before she married she wasn't exactly a wild and reckless high-society girl. Her husband had been the bachelor at the next farm down and had one day just up and asked her out of the blue if she wanted to get married; she asked when and he said, "Well, I gotta go to town this Saturday anyways," and four days later she was a wife. And later a mom and when in due course the nest emptied, a bookkeeper.

She bought two reams of typing paper, a pad of carbon paper, and new ribbons for the forty-year-old Smith Corona from her high school days. The ribbons were almost impossible to find, but Jack at the Variety Store found a carton of them in his storeroom. Sold them all to her for a dollar.

Glenda sat in the spare bedroom and wrote about luxurious hotels she'd never seen, darkly handsome men she'd never met, and nights so wild she marveled that her imagination could create them. Her women were sexy with a capital *S* and her men were loving with a capital *L*. And her novel was soon going nowhere with a capital *N*.

The problem was not her lack of experience or questions of spelling or grammar—the typewriter was just so slow that while her words were describing the heroine's gown, Glenda's brain already had her tumbling on the bed with Derek and the gown was nowhere in sight. Every missed key or clumsy adjective would be another stoppage, a roadblock to be dismantled, and repairs to be made.

She knew of the technology available to writers and she asked Eva one day, casually, if she could ride along to the mall in St. Cloud the next time she went in. In a few days' time she had laid down thirteen hundred dollars for a computer and printer; the salesman said he would deliver it and set it up.

"Good God!" is how she put it after struggling to grasp even the most basic notions; it was more difficult to understand than anything she ever encountered in high school or at the feed mill. Her characters lay abandoned, nearly forgotten between ink and pixel, lost to a world of icons, mice, parallel ports, dialog boxes, RAMs and ROMs and megabytes, left clicks, right clicks, and double clicks. She came close to tears nearly every day.

After a month of watching her suffer Eva said her uncle Marvin had left an Olivetti word processor that he had used for a long time. It was just taking up space and she was sure Aunt Ruth would let her have it for nothing. Far simpler than a computer, she said.

The computer and printer already took up most of the space on Glenda's desk, and when Eva brought over the word processor with its printer it covered all the rest. The little notebook where she wrote her ideas had to sit on a skinny place at the side of the desk and the Smith Corona sat on the floor. Her spare bedroom now looked like a full-grown office.

The printer turned out beautiful copy for a few days and then the ink seemed to thin out, and as Lavendula headed into an ecstatic frenzy on her kitchen floor and Derek tore at his belt, the words paled into whiteness as if censored by an unseen force, and the machine would write no more. Robert came over. "Too old," he said, looking over cartridges and spools and small metal pieces. "Too old to find parts, but I'll try." Nothing in St. Cloud, and phone calls to office supply stores in Minneapolis were futile as well. Too old, at barely twenty.

So Glenda found herself back at the computer store, where they offered to take back her computer in trade on a new little model that came in a variety of colors. But the trade-in they offered was so low she decided to get the new, far less complicated one and keep the first one so that she could use that after she mastered the simpler one. "I just have to get used to it," she said.

She moved the library table into the spare bedroom to hold the new machine and the printer, put a cover on the first computer, and set the word processor and its printer beside that, just in case Robert ever found parts for it.

The salesman had also sold her a *For Dummies* manual, which he said would be helpful to her in learning this newest computer. She remembered her dad saying to her once, "If you think you're a dummy, you'll be a dummy." She had misgivings.

She read, and she tried to follow and to understand, but when she started on the keyboard, letters, numbers, symbols, and designs seemed to flow across the screen in uncontrollable ways. The machine would ask questions like DO YOU WANT TO SAVE SEPTEMBER? when she didn't even know it was in danger, and she would sit stunned. Warnings that the computer had performed an illegal action would appear, and she would anticipate a total crash of the entire house of pixels. Pages of type would unexpectedly disappear. Sometimes as she stared at the screen she was sure she heard a low laugh coming from somewhere in the black heart at the center of the machine. Sometimes the mocking laughter got so loud she would shut down everything with the OFF switch, forsaking the EXIT process. Another chapter gone off into the ether. One late night she was sure she heard "Bury Me Not Under the Weeping Willow," a song she hadn't thought about in thirty years.

Kind Eva came to her rescue again. "You just write your story, honey. Write it on lined paper with a number two pencil, and I'll type it for you and I'll never say a word to anyone."

A word about what, Glenda wondered, my computer ineptitude or my smutty characters? But she was deflated to the point where she agreed and began to write on a legal pad.

Her bold and reckless characters, however, turned to jelly when they knew they were being watched. They seemed to be terrified of Eva. They began speaking like business acquaintances and rarely took their clothes off, even to sleep. A tryst became dull as a meeting of highway engineers. Robert took a look at the ongoing work and said it was worthless and told Eva she was wasting her time copying it. She said she thought the same thing but the poor woman had put her heart and soul and worse than that, her money, into writing this book. He said she was doing her no favors by helping her and in fact was only making it worse because sooner or later she would have to face the disaster anyway. Cut the losses, he said.

Eva said Maybe we could find some new word processor and give it to her as a retirement gift. She could handle that word processor; the printer was the problem. So Robert searched the Web and found they still made word processors and they weren't that expensive and seven days later a UPS truck pulled up in Glenda's yard.

Freed from weeks of repression, the predatory Derek and the vulnerable Lavendula, voluptuous Shirelle and idealistic Jeremy, the slut Veronica, the mystic Alphonso, and the evil Marsten Poltroon are back to steamy cavorting, craven scheming, and living boundless life to its reckless and uninhibited fullness, all springing from the north wall of a small rural bedroom lined with eight machines: two word processors, two computers, three printers, and an antique Smith Corona. The author views this battery of literary gear not as defeat but as lending an air of authority to the vivid prose springing so lightly and swiftly forth. She has already finished the last chapter wherein she dramatically and gratuitously murders a couple of minor characters she had come to dislike and then completely buries a long and razor-sharp ivory-handled Damascus carving blade, still warm with the juices of a delicious roast stag, between the ribs under the upraised left arm of Poltroon, who was just then proclaiming another toast to his own success and hoisting a glass of indescribably delicious royal Spanish red wine from the king's own cellars. She is now concentrating on the late middle game where she makes the connections and ties up the loose ends, and in the process vividly portrays another wild romping.

Sex, violence, intrigue, and passion in lush climates; luxury hotels, elegant mansions, steaming marketplaces, and vile and dangerous back streets, all spilling from a retired bookkeeper who spent her working life in a worn wood office on a flat landscape, towered over by large vertical shafts holding hundreds of tons of corn, oats, barley, and wheat, and wherefrom the single small window looked out on only dusty grain trucks and a few pigeons.

We are still wondering how this may turn out. If she finds a good agent and all goes well it might someday sit on shelves in airport bookstores around the world. And folks in her hometown will look at her—and her husband—in an entirely different light.

10

THE SECRET CHAMP

WE STARTED THE 2000s WITH A SIX-WEEK stand in St. Paul and then in late February flew to Scotland and Ireland, where my dad had spent a short time before flying off to North Africa in World War II; a place he spoke of fondly. Ireland, that is, not North Africa. We did three shows over there with rental equipment, at Limerick, Dublin, and Edinburgh. We didn't need a truck but they took me along anyway, just out of habit. Got back in early March, took a few weeks off, and then brought the show gear to New York for another four weeks at Town Hall, our East Coast hideout. Drove home and four weeks later returned to New York, where I picked it all back up and set out for California, to Pasadena and Redding.

While getting the truck underway for the long haul to the other coast, it occurred to me that one word best fitting a semi is *ponderous*. It's a good word because it sounds like what it means. It could have been conceived with the future eighteen-wheeler in mind. Drivers who wear cowboy gear are somewhat aside of the mark, sartorially, because the rig is a lot closer to an elephant than it is to a cow pony. And I'm not an expert on what elephant drivers are wearing these days; for all I know they could be in cowboy boots themselves, and blue jeans and big silver belt buckles. But even the elephant is a ballerina compared to a tractor-trailer. Bib overalls and feed caps might be closer to a correct fashion statement, given the size of the machinery, but truckers generally see themselves as too footloose to dress like farmers. (Except of course for those truckers who actually *are* farmers, or at least were.)

But the everyday reality of it is that drivers these days don't wear as much cowboy gear as they used to. They wear ordinary cheap work shirts and jeans, and either sneakers or round-toed boots. The duded-up pointy-toed trucker in a cowboy hat is becoming somewhat of a rarity. Some don't even bother to make up a handle for the CB.

They call Pasadena subtropical and semiarid, and it snowed there only twice in recorded history, in 1932 and 1949. Home to the Jet Propulsion Laboratory, Cal Tech, the American Academy of Dramatic Arts, the Mount Wilson Observatory, and the amazing Huntington Library—five million works cataloged there.

And bless their hearts, it's the birthplace of the freeway, expanded now from the old Arroyo Seco Parkway which ran nine miles from downtown Pasadena to downtown

Los Angeles without a traffic light or a cross street. It's home also to the Rose Bowl, which nearly disappears into the green and leafy neighborhood. Beautiful houses, beautiful downtown, amazing trees. It's basically paradise.

Paradise is of course no place for a trucker. On the other hand, the freeway is, and when I read a folk music critic moaning about "a suburbanized and sanitized America . . . a giant crowded highway lined end to end with Wal-Mart and McDonald's . . . the increasingly vulgar and distracted audience" for which today's radio is targeted, and longing for "an age when life was slower, folks knew each other, and decent, unpretentious music could be found just about anywhere," well, it just sort of set me off a little.

Because I spend a good deal of time in exactly that environment, and I grew up in that previous decent and unpretentious age when folks knew each other. And I'll admit the giant crowded highway isn't always pretty, at least not compared to the crowded city markets in exotic *National Geographic* places like Algiers, but at the same time there's less crime on the giant highway and you can take care of business and move on, and most of us who aren't truckers can get off the giant highway fairly quickly and into a quiet neighborhood of our choosing.

So I have to get up and speak for wide highways lined with commercial vulgarity everywhere: They're as natural as the carotids and the femorals and the aortas we all carry around, folks. They work well at what they do, if you don't jam them up with tollbooths, and if the view is a little too jarring for the sensitive types, the hidden beauty of the eight-lane and the four-lane and the cloverleaf is exactly that they are a magnet for all that nasty commercialism. It used to attach itself to the two-lanes; now the interstates have taken it on themselves, not only the rampant garishness strewn around but also all the heavy traffic, all those monster semis like ours, and the buses—not to mention all those millions of grim commuters—so that almost anywhere in America you can cruise back roads as sweet as maple syrup and rarely have to come face to face with a Peterbilt largecar.

The net result of the concentration is that this country is more beautiful now than it's been since the early mud-road era. You can ride the backcountry of Montana and Wyoming or any state you please and you will be astounded at how peaceful it all is. You can hit a deer in any state with little concern of being rear-ended when, too late, you slam on the brakes. I encourage people to go and enjoy it, away from the trucks and the runaway ugliness of the giant highway. Hell, bring your guitar.

And when it comes right down to it, of course, it's all one road. It has a hundred thousand names and numbers and millions of mileposts, and it's everything from ten lanes of concrete stacked four high to a couple of tracks in the woods, but when you're on the road, your road *is* the road. All the ones that join from the sides, coming in from what-all and heading off to who-cares, they don't count. You don't see it like they do from the airplane, all that gridwork and those big turnpikes slithering off in those other directions. When you talk about the road, you talk about your own road. If someone's gotta go down the road it's not the same route as someone else's gotta go down the road, but it's still the same road. Both metaphorically and physically. No matter where it goes, it's all one road.

The first song ever written was probably about love, but I'd bet the second one was about the road. Merle Haggard put it about as right as anybody ever did in "White Line Fever." That line about the wrinkles in his forehead showing the miles he left behind him.

I left paradise for Redding (where Merle lives) on Sunday morning, looking forward to some hot bleak desert and some hardscrabble farms and fading small towns. The ride up through the Central Valley fit that bill just right, a progression from the barren wire-strewn foothills of the San Gabriels, where steel towers held long catenaries of fat power lines high above abandoned barbed wire, onto a hard flatland fed with enough water from distant unseen mountains to grow cotton and vegetables. I took Highway 99 because I heard it was a good road, a low-lying four-lane that doesn't suffer the truck pounding that Interstate 5 gets and is therefore in better shape. I went that way to do my part to equalize the pounding. In Bakersfield it crossed Buck Owens Boulevard and I could see the Buck Owens Crystal Palace there off to the right, a bright-painted Branson kind of Opry House in the middle of town. I've heard they have good steaks there.

North of there it was 250 miles of weary farmland to Sacramento; towns just hanging on, a few odd businesses along the road, like Pallets Bought and Sold, where disordered stacks of bleached pallets looked like they'd never move again; Used Equipment Bought and Sold, where four thirty-year-old International dump trucks sat with cracked glass and bad tires, a place on the cusp between a dealership and a junkyard; and then We Buy And Sell Horses, not that different from the Pallets and the Used Equipment. I saw old corrals and dispirited animals, the barn door hanging loose, the house long past needing paint. Even the trees seem tired, leaves hanging straight down, branches sagging.

A municipal sign said WELCOME TO MCFARLAND—THE HEARTBEAT OF AGRICULTURE. It looked as if they got enough water to scratch out a living but not much more. I once pictured the Central Valley as sort of an Iowa without winter, but the word *lush* did not come to mind as I passed the towns of Pixley and Tipton and Tulare, towns with open land between buildings, the land flat and hard. Scraps of debris here and there. Must be tough on teenagers. Not much to do, heat blazing down, the temptation of Hollywood barely a half day's drive down the road.

A sign read HOUSE MOVING AND RAISING; two old wrecks of houses sat up on heavy blocking in a yard. Eight-wheel bogies and a couple of despondent trucks with winches coiled loose in rusty cable sat there in the sun. There were also new ag buildings along the road, with bright blue framing and gleaming new galvanized metal siding and a lot of straight and curved tubular grain chutes, these all looking efficient and purposeful.

Saw new orchards laid out on land literally as flat as a pool table, so that water could run down every row and make it all the way to the end. Young orchards seemed laid out with a laser, the alignment so accurate there were straight lines not just at the forty-five- and ninety-degree angles but also at four different points in between; I counted seven straight lines running off to the distance at each field. There is a strange paradox in an orchard: You can be in complete shade among hundreds of trees there and yet with not a single place to hide.

The highway went on up through the little burgs of Visalia, Goshen, Selma, Parlier, Fowler. I passed Fresno and crossed the San Joaquin River into Madera County, on up through Chowchilla and Merced, Turlock and Modesto, and Lodi and Galt, and the land darkened with moisture. Leaving the hardness of cotton country seemed to bring on more fun: A sign on a tavern said BAR ROOM DANCING. In the distance I saw downtown Sacramento and farther north I passed flooded fields divided with rice-paddy berms. The machinery in the fields became larger, with big dual tires like balloons.

There were small churches with strange names among the trailer courts and orchards and cotton fields of the Central Valley. The Celebrate Life Church and the Church of Glad Tidings and all kinds of Baptists. A billboard said HELL HAS NO EXIT; READ LUKE 3:16 TO END; another, at the Victory Chapel, said, BE NOT DECEIVED, good advice in any situation. A frequently repeated sign, put there by a growers' coalition, read: FOOD GROWS WHERE WATER FLOWS. There were at least six of those between Bakersfield and Yuba City. A large carved wooden sign in a farmer's yard:

TRY PRUNES
THEY'RE GOOD

Left the rice country and forty miles north of Sacramento crossed the Feather River at an elevation of sixty feet above sea level. Then began a long gradual rise to Yuba City and Chico, and the orchards became dramatically thicker and signs appeared for walnuts and cherries. It was Mother's Day, and it had begun to rain lightly; in the fading afternoon I saw in a dark green graveyard beneath monumental trees two well-dressed men walking side by side, heading slowly back to a car in the low moody light. They looked like brothers, maybe even twins. It was a striking scene, and I felt fortunate to be in a truck, high enough to see over fences and hedges. I pictured their mother, and thought of the comfort of cemeteries.

The ride from there to Redding went through lush orchard country, olives and walnuts and almonds. I arrived to a city crowded with pickup trucks, there for the Redding Rodeo; I could hear it and smell it, and it sounded good and smelled nostalgic, to a flatlander.

On the place mat at the J & W Truck Stop it said that Redding was the northernmost point in the Western Hemisphere where a palm tree would grow. Some people still make a living by panning gold in the nearby mountains. A local goldsmith named Carpenter said that in 1995 a man walked into their Olde West shop with a fifteen-ounce gold nugget taken from French Gulch, not that far away; it was worth nine thousand dollars. In the town of Paradise, east of Chico, there was once found a gold nugget weighing fifty-four pounds.

A young man from this area, born in a place called Somes Bar out there on the far side of Siskiyou County, was drafted into the army during World War II. He was told to write his birthplace on a form and wrote "Somes Bar, in California," but the second "s" was not quite legible and the desk sergeant thought he'd written "Some Bar in California" and had him tossed in the brig for being a wise guy.

Mount Shasta stood gleaming white in the sun, sixty miles away to the northwest, and it looked close, and off to the east stood Mount Lassen, still considered an active volcano. It blew dramatically in 1914 and could do the same again any minute, and what a treat to live with that sitting out there like a loaded cannon, reminding you that life is short and anything can happen so you'd better enjoy it while you've got it. Ten miles away the Shasta Dam, built in 1938, holds back the Sacramento to form crystal-blue Lake Shasta; when it's full it holds more than six billion tons of water, or about six thousand gallons for every inhabitant of the United States.

They are an independent sort up here, and quick to point out that this is the real northern California. San Francisco, Sacramento, the Napa Valley, Oakland; that's *all* southern California. The area has a long history of secessionist movements, the most recent a ballot initiative in 1992. They are persistently hopeful they can break free.

While I was in Redding I looked up a guy I'd gone to college with in North Dakota, an architect. His name is Leighton and he told me a story about a fellow he'd grown up with who had died a few months earlier, a guy named Dennis. Dennis lived in a small house in a small town in Nebraska; he himself was not all that big either. He never married. Leighton went back to the town for the funeral and stayed on for a couple of weeks with relatives. The day they auctioned off the belongings it rained all morning and through most of the afternoon.

He said there was a corner cabinet, good sized and nicely made but not a store-bought piece. It had seven shelves, a shelf for each of his seven sisters. On each shelf there were two or three pictures of that sister, and some small gifts that she had sent him. A small bronze horse; a card with a print of a famous moody painting; a small wooden boat model. An ashtray from Acapulco, a miniature clock from Austria, a brass Empire State Building. The best things were the portraits of the sisters, taken in the '40s and '50s and each showing the woman as glamorous as a small-town portrait studio of that time could make her. Over-the-shoulder shots, Marlene Dietrich looks, head-tilted-back Lana Turner poses. Dresses that hung like drapes.

It was at the urging of two of his sisters that Dennis had bought this house. He had been renting a room above the hardware store for four or five years and had saved enough money for a down payment, but couldn't of his own just go find a house to live in. As the only brother, the girls looked out for him. They found this small and almost elegant cottage before it even came on the market. After they took him to the house he was filled with the wonder of it. He said to Leighton: "The house is nice. It has curtains at the windows and everything. It even has a doorbell."

Dennis had never pictured himself owning anything like this. He lived a tidy life and had no grand aspirations. He kept his black Dodge business coupe always shining; you'd seldom see dust on it. Going to get gas or groceries was to him almost a formal occasion. He worked as the county surveyor, had an office at the courthouse and a county truck, and used the Dodge for errands and on the weekends. He was a regular at happy hour at the Nile Bar downtown, usually on Monday, Thursday, and Friday, and would put more than his share into the jukebox.

Leighton said, "Music, especially country music, made him happy. On weekends he'd drive to someplace that had a band, places like small-town saloons or a country dance hall. Sometimes he'd drive to Lincoln for a Willie Nelson or a Waylon Jennings concert. 'I follow the music,' he'd say, 'I go where the music leads me.' On vacations he saw the country stars, Merle, Johnny Cash, Chet Atkins, Hank Snow. The Louvin Brothers, Loretta Lynn, Tammy Wynette. Wanted to see George Jones but he never did."

He was unafraid of bars and of strangers. He was compact and wiry and had a certain look that even hostile drunks didn't challenge. No one in his town knew him to be a fighter except by the rumor that he'd been in the navy and been at sea on a heavy cruiser and was on the ship's boxing team. Some said that he had been the fleet welterweight champion.

He'd never deny or confirm any of it. Someone would say, So I heard you used to box a little, and he'd say, Where'd you hear a thing like that?

Oh, couple guys were talkin' in here the other night when the boxing was on TV. Said you were on the navy boxing team, somethin' like that?

People say all kinds of things, I guess. You don't want to believe anything of what you hear and only half of what you see. You don't happen to have a light, do you?

The guy might light his cigarette and say, So is that true? Did you ever do any boxing?

Like I said, you don't want to believe too much of what

you hear in this place. I've told a few whoppers myself, haha. Thanks for the light. And if he sensed the guy wasn't going to let up he'd go to the jukebox.

He was a good dancer and was able to meet the ladies, but if he had a steady girlfriend no one seemed to know about it. He would sometimes be gone for a weekend but when asked he would say he was on a fishing trip or had been to a concert. He had been out and around all the way to the last couple of years, when he'd suffered a series of strokes.

Leighton said the auction was a quiet affair, not many buyers. The auctioneer began to offer blocks of related items—for instance, all the kitchen chairs and the table—at low opening bids. Leighton ended up with the old steamer trunk and all its contents for fourteen dollars. A cursory look revealed only fabrics, blankets and table-cloths and the like, but he had dug in there and knew the lower third of it to be papers and photographs.

At the house where he was staying he found at the very bottom of the trunk an album chronicling the life of a younger woman in town whom Leighton knew, Anna Mae Martinson. From the faded birth notice in the paper in 1959 through high school graduation in 1977 and into marriage and children, with miscellaneous clippings and photos along the way. There were no actual photographic prints; this was a life observed from some distance, mainly through the local paper, formal announcements, and yearbooks. He wondered at the connection; he had also been a regular at the Nile happy hour and had never heard Dennis even mention Anna Mae.

Four of the seven sisters were still alive and the youngest, Joanne, had been the closest to the sailor. Leighton called her and asked if she'd have coffee with him. She would, and after the customary exchange of small-town news and speculation he said, "I suppose you know I bought your brother's steamer trunk?"

"Yes, I do."

"Do you know of any reason why he would be interested in Anna Mae Martinson?"

"Why do you ask?"

"Well, there were a lot of pictures of her in that trunk."

She looked at him for a long time. "I didn't know that, or I would have bought it myself . . . Hm. I suppose . . . the only way I can answer that . . . and I need you to keep quiet . . . is to tell you. Because if I don't, you'll start asking everyone else around and then the gossip will start flying. You know how that is. But if I do tell you the truth, can I trust that it not to go any farther than the two of us?"

"I promise. You can trust me."

"Well, I hope so. There's nothing for you to gain by blabbing anyway, other than just being an old gossip."

"That's right. I can keep quiet when I want to. And I live a long ways away. And Dennis was my friend."

She took a breath. "Anna Mae Martinson would be shocked to know this, but she is my niece."

Leighton said he just sat there for a minute. "Your brother . . . he . . . ?"

"That's right. He never told a single soul, not even me. I found out from Anna's mother, one of my best friends. She was engaged to Roger Martinson; he was the only man she had ever dated. They were 'saving themselves for marriage,' as they used to say. My brother had signed up for the navy. They were at a dance. They went out to his car. Things got out of control and later, when she thought there might be a baby on the way, he demanded that she break with Roger and marry him instead and she was so mixed up and angry at herself and at him she said something like 'no way in hell.' But I believe he truly loved her and couldn't stand the idea of not being with her.

"Anyway, he shipped out soon after and she married Roger and never told him and they had a slightly premature girl. I don't think my brother ever recovered from that. He never approached Anna Mae, as far as I know, but he obviously watched over her. It must have eaten at him something terrible, all those years."

Leighton said, "I bet it did. It must have been real hell sometimes, like at graduation."

"Yes, and sometimes I think he'd just leave town for a while and try to get away from it."

They sat. "Something else I was wondering about, if you don't mind . . . the rumors about your brother being a boxer . . . is there any truth to them?"

"He was the welterweight champion of the Sixth Fleet, and he went on to become the welterweight champion of the U.S. Navy. I was the only one he told about that. I always felt it was Anna Mae's mother who drove him to that . . . I think he always thought that he was getting into the ring with Roger Martinson. And he never lost a fight."

Leighton said to me, "I can't help but wonder if Anna Mae would be proud to know that her father was the welterweight champ of the whole navy. But if anyone tells her, it'll have to be her mother."

* * *

I left Redding Sunday morning heading east into the Lassen National Forest and drove through a fabulous series of panoramas, from dense woods opening onto still ponds, rising to evergreens and high meadows, rising higher to mountain peaks, descending into great spreading valleys of light and color and distant cattle. Each of these scenes seemed to have a narrow passage leading to it, some notch ahead in the woods or a shallow pass through a ridge miles ahead, and they carried from one beautiful expanse into another, like a series of rooms in a museum of natural history. Only better. I arrived on Interstate 80 at Reno, crossed the vastness of Nevada past the Great Salt Lake and turned north on I–15, through the ankle of Idaho to Butte, and then boogied on east, through Montana, North Dakota, and Minnesota. Not much traffic, good weather all the way, and what a great way to end a trip.

11

FIGHTIN' WORDS

BACK IN THE EARLY '80s A BUNCH OF US began to ride Harleys for the annual Sturgis Bike Rally in western South Dakota. From the west side of the Black Hills we could see the Bighorn Mountains in Wyoming standing out there like a flatlander's dream. After one ride through the high meadows and steep canyons we've been out to the Rocky Mountains every summer since, not so much to the Sturgis rally anymore but all over the rest of it, sometimes running as far south as the Four Corners by Durango and as far west as the Snake River in Idaho. We stay away from the helmet states on the coast, but there is more than enough drama out west without having to go that far. And nobody needs that West Coast traffic and all those cops, anyway.

On a blazing hot afternoon that summer my pal Jim and I were riding south through the high hard plains in central Wyoming, heading down from Livingston, Montana, through Cody to Laramie. The radio show was scheduled there the following spring, so we called this a scouting mission. It was 105 degrees that day. When the air's hotter than your own self it doesn't cool you to ride faster. It heats you up, like a convection oven. We stopped in Thermopolis for a beer to interrupt the cooking process.

There were only a few in the saloon, a small group of rancher types down at the far end and a white-haired man on a stool at the middle of the bar by himself. The guy was wrinkled and sunbaked, clean shaven, gnarled hands around his beer glass. I guessed him to be maybe sixty-five years old. Probably five-nine or five-ten, maybe a lean 170 pounds. He was wearing jeans and a cotton shirt and an engineer's cap, the typical striped blue railroad cap. We sat a couple of stools away.

We ordered a couple of tall ones, which we emptied and had refilled before we even took time to grin. After we settled in the old man turned to us and offered, in a voice that was raspy but without animosity: "You fellas wanna fight?"

There was a pause. We looked at him to see if this was a joke.

"Fight?" I said, wondering if there was something about us that offended the man, like the fact that we weren't cowboys.

"Yeah. Go out in back and throw some punches."

Jim said, "What. We just got here. What's the problem?"

"No problem," the man said, "I jist wondered if you fellas wanted to out in back and do a little fighting."

Jim said, "Well, not really, I guess. I'm not really in a fighting mood, myself; not yet, anyway."

"No, me neither," I said, "Don't need a fight right now." I almost said *But if I did you'd be the first guy I'd ask,* but thought better of it. Careful not to get sarcastic; he could be stone damn crazy. We acted as though it was a reasonable offer and perhaps even a friendly overture and we appreciated it, but the time just wasn't right. I looked around to see if there was an option, maybe a pool table.

The man looked at us, one to another, gauging us, and then shrugged his shoulders and said, "Okay."

He went back to his beer. An awkward moment. I thought maybe we should say we didn't mean to be unneighborly or anything. On the other hand we didn't want to appear faint of heart either. But we'd backed away from a challenge.

Somehow it stands to reason that if you get in a fight you ought to fight to win, whatever it takes, and it's not something a sensible person would undertake without some purpose, be it practical or on principle, or both. It was hotter than the hinges of hell outside; why would anybody think it would be a good time to out there and fight? I thought of saying something like "Now, if I had some reason to fight, I'd do it . . . if I really hated your guts or something, I'd be all for it . . ."

We should have done the honest thing and said what we were both thinking: "Hell no. What kind of a dumb question is that, mister?" After a rejection the moment for explanation doesn't last long, though, and we quickly had nothing to do but to go back to our beer and keep to ourselves. It seemed we'd been tested and found wanting. But there were only three realistic outcomes in that offer and none held any appeal: Ride into a small town and beat the crap out of an old man; ride into a small town and have the crap beat out of us by an old man; or ride into town and have the crap beat out of us by an old man and his rancher pals. And then get tossed in the tank for being disorderly.

If we'd stayed for a while and had more beer we might have started a conversation and maybe we'd have heard some stories, or maybe there would have been a fight after all. But we drank up and rode on to Laramie, vaguely unsettled.

Back on the road I thought of any number of guys I knew who would have said, "Hell yes, let's go! C'mon, you skinny old fart, let's see whatcha got! I could use a good fight." Thought about when I was in college and worked a couple of summers on a section gang for the Northern Pacific Railroad in my hometown in North Dakota. The job attracted a number of interesting characters, not the least of whom were the Vanson boys, Dean and Gene, whom I had known at a distance in high school. They were tough and rangy and had reputations as fighters who would take on guys of any size or disposition. After working with them for a while I got to like them both. They worked hard and had a certain harsh Scandinavian humor.

One Friday night I was having a couple of beers with Gene in Polly's Lounge and he said, in that clipped way he and his brother had: "I kicked the shit out a big farmer up there at the bar in St. Thomas the other night."

"You got into it with some guy at the Warsaw Dance Hall last Saturday, too, didn't you?" I said. "Didn't you tell me that?"

"Yeah. Busted his nose. That was about all he wanted, too."

I said, friendly like, "Man, you get in more fights than anybody I know. How come you're always fightin' somebody?"

He bristled. "Well. A man's got to defend his honor." He looked at me as if exactly such a moment might be at hand.

"Well, right," I said, "but the average man isn't called upon to defend his honor two or three times a week." I was smiling when I said this, hoping I wasn't impugning his honor right then.

He thought about it for a minute and then brightened

and smiled and said, with his characteristic honesty, "It's fun to fight."

Maybe it is, if you're good at it. Maybe that stringy old man in Thermopolis was some relative of his, too. And if he was, I'm glad we avoided him. But if I'd have been Gene Vanson I probably would have simply decked that old fool right there, just for the fun of it.

We gassed up in Casper and arrived in Laramie about six, our ears fried bacon-crisp and gullets parched like dried salt flats, only to find closed-down rowdiness and spruced-up gentrification. On a downtown cowboy bar a genuine neon rodeo bronc and rider hung dusty and unlit in midbuck over double doors nailed shut behind plywood. Real discouraging it was, the thought of trying to slake a manly thirst on a microbrew or a glass of Peeno Greezio—discouraging until we hit the Buckhorn, that is.

The Buckhorn made up for a lot of sins of good taste and high tone simply by being a real working bar. It looked like a bar, was beat to hell like a bar, had bar graffiti carved into the furniture and real bullet holes in the walls. Nothing fake about that circular fracture in the mirror over the bartender's head, either. He said it had come from a .270 Winchester fired from across the street in 1976, and the fellow who fired it had been rejected by the lady who was bartending at the time—at least that's how

I remember the story. At his trial the guy said he wasn't shooting at her and he wasn't trying to kill anyone in particular but he sort of meant to kill somebody. Didn't much matter who it was. At least not at that moment. In other words he didn't actually have a specific figure in the sights, so it was a cross between a practical joke and attempted murder, and he was glad, once he cooled off, that nobody got hurt.

There were also some bullet holes in the vicinity of the wrecked pay phone, more recent ones, from a revolver. The bartender said a lot of that sort of feistiness has let up in recent years but you never know, folks get crazy sometimes. There were a lot of dusty critters' heads mounted way up there on the high walls, near the original metal ceiling. Elk, deer, bighorn sheep, coyote, bear, mountain lion, bobcat, and hawk, all gazing off to the distance as if contemplating life's ironies. Including their own.

There was a carved back bar with the aforementioned high mirrors, and a scarred and beaten mahogany main bar; nobody ever took a notion to update the place. It had been in the family for generations. The owner's grandfather was never bothered by the fighting that used to go on in there; in fact, he said, if there hadn't been a fight for a while the old man would come around the bar and start one himself.

Jim said to me, "Speaking of fighting, y'know that old

bastard back there in Thermopolis?"

"Yeah."

"I think I figured it out. I'm thinkin' the guy is probably some crazy old bull rider. Maybe he misses getting knocked around. Maybe fun to a guy like that has to be somethin' dangerous that ends up okay at the end. Or at least ends up where you're glad to still be alive, y'know?"

"Well, you could be onto something there, mister."

"And that cap—maybe he's a bull rider who doesn't wear a cowboy hat anymore. Maybe he's sick of tourists or something."

"I could see that. And if you're an old bull rider almost anything that's not bull riding is probably fun. Maybe just falling off the back of a pickup would be fun, compared to riding one of those crazy-ass bulls. At least the pickup won't come back and put a horn in your liver."

Jim said, "Yeah. Fighting bare fisted would be nothing. Maybe fighting with tire irons would even be fun, hell, to a guy like that."

"And the guy could have been an old railroader, too. He had the cap. I knew some real fighters when I worked on the section gang."

"Next time we go through there we should check up on that guy."

"Yeah."

When we weren't thirsty anymore we went and found a

couple of motel rooms, cruised Main Street, found steak, and ended up back at the Buckhorn. They had a terrific rock band in the back room that night. Can't remember the name of it, but I can still hear it and still see a couple of those ladies on the dance floor. Those jeans.

We went east and north from Laramie and stopped at a lodge near Newcastle, Wyoming, where the owner was a friend of friends and treated us like kings. Next day we rode in and around the Black Hills and stayed in Spearfish and then headed back to Minnesota, ahead of the rush to the annual Sturgis rally. We later heard there were five hundred thousand bikers there that year.

The coming of a new fall season brought to mind a man named Howard who'd gone to Houston the previous November to visit his uncle Ray and maybe even to find work down there. Get away from Minnesota for a winter, he said, see how the warmer half lives. He found Ray's place on a Wednesday evening and the two of them had a beer and talked about family jokes and jokers; the short-sheeting, the fake documents, the fake snake in the silverware drawer, the mouse in the couch. The carefully aimed garden hose in the bush, suddenly activated at a barbecue. The elaborate hoaxes they had pulled on each other, fake notices from the sheriff and all that, and how everyone in the family looks in their shoes before they put them on, all traceable to Ray's mother's side.

Talk turned to the neighbor directly to the east, an ordinary house but with raw junk strewn all around; he asked how it was living next to all that. Ray said they were good neighbors but their yard was an unholy mess. Car hulks and old lawn mowers, worn tires and appliance carcasses, piles of soggy mattresses, broken lamps; overstuffed chairs with the upholstery coming out.

"It looks bad now and it's worse in the daylight. But y'know, the guy's a really good guy, and his wife's a peach, too, and they've got a couple of kids, heck, you couldn't ask for nicer kids than that. I don't know what it is, why they let stuff pile up like that. They're good people. Honest people, straighforward. He's a no-bullshit kinda guy. His name is Henry Coble."

"So I don't suppose you'd ever talk to 'em about it."

"Oh no. I mean, he's even mentioned it to me a couple of times, that he'd like to clean the place up, but I just nod. I'd never think of telling him to clean it up."

"Maybe we could pull a trick on him. You got a suit around here? And a necktie?"

"I suppose I could find one . . . been kind of a long time. What you gonna do?"

"I could get all suited up and go over there tomorrow

and say I'm from the city inspection department and he's gotta clean his yard up or we're gonna have to give him a ticket, somethin' like that."

"He didn't see you drive in?"

"Well, I don't think so. He sure didn't see my face in the dark."

Ray thought about it. "Y'know, if he didn't kill you on the spot, that'd be a good one. It'll get his back up, for sure. Let 'im stew for a day or two and then maybe have 'im over for barbecue or something, and then bring you in and tell 'im you're my nephew from Wisconsin, the new guy working for the city. Could be kind of a hoot."

So Thursday morning about ten o'clock Howie left by the side door and walked west and up around the block, so as to approach the place from the other side. The old suit was creased sideways from uninterrupted years of hanging in the closet, and not a perfect fit or the latest in fashion. But so much the better. He knocked on the door and a large swarthy bearded man in long hair and a tie-dyed T-shirt answered.

"Mr. Coble?"

"Maybe. Who are you?" His eyes were narrowed and his rough face showed not a trace of neighborliness.

"I'm Andres Martin, with the City of Houston Building Inspection Department."

"Uh-huh. You got some kinda problem? I mean, other than you're workin' for the city?"

"No problem at all, sir. We're doing an informal neighborhood observation, not really an inspection but just kind of an overview."

"You're not from Texas, are you?" His face was red and his voice was what they call gravelly.

"Nosir. I'm from Wisconsin. I just work for the City of Houston, is all. Sure is warm down here, and I'll tell you what, I'm glad to be away from those crazy winters up there."

"Uh-huh . . . I see them zero numbers on TV and I say, ain't no way. No way."

"It does get cold, and slidin' around on the ice gets old after a few years, too."

"I expect that's prob'ly true . . . So: Maybe you don't mind this kinda stuff up where you come from, but somebody musta already told you that folks down here don't much appreciate people comin' in and tellin' 'em what to do, 'specially on their own property. Nothin' personal against you, but they prob'ly sent you out here and figgered somebody'd take a shot atcha and they'd have a good laugh back at the office. I'm just sayin' this for yer own good, you understand. I got nothin' against northerners myself."

"Yessir. And I know what you're talking about, and I'm

not out to issue any tickets or any orders of any kind."

"Glad to hear it. Long as I'm payin' these crazy high taxes here the city's got no business tellin' me what it oughta look like. Men fought and died for stuff like that."

"Yessir."

Coble said, "You must be here for somethin', though. City didn't send you over here to talk about the weather, did they."

"Ah; no. And yes, I do have to tell you your yard isn't exactly in compliance with the current ordinances, and you could maybe save yourself some trouble down the road if you hauled those cars away and got rid of the refrigerators and stoves and the furniture and the tubs and all rest of it out there. Like I said, I'm not even issuing you a warning. Just a little friendly advice. Off the record, before the real Texans come by." He smiled.

"Friendly advice, huh? Well it don't sound friendly to me . . . but I might think about it . . . and on the other hand I might jist wait until they do come around. I might git the fellas from the paper down here, and the TV station. Talk about the Constitution, maybe about the right to privacy and life and liberty and all that. Talk about citizens in a so-called free society. I been here a long time and nobody ever complained before. And hell, I could jist move away and leave it; I don't need to live in this damn place . . . 'specially if the gestapo are out to straighten everybody out . . ."

"Nobody's made any complaint at all, Mr. Coble, and we don't mean it to get that way, either. I'm not here in regard to any complaint from anybody, because there was no complaint."

"Uh-huh . . . Jist out walkin' around and doin' good, I guess? Savin' good citizens from low-down criminals like me?"

"Nosir. It's more like trying to save the city money by not having to take legal action. I don't much like the idea of being a do-gooder, either."

"Well if you ain't a do-gooder, I'd say you're mighty close. Looks like you'd do till one comes along."

"Yessir. Well, thanks for your time."

"Right." Coble gave him a hard and sour look and slowly closed the door.

Howie left walking east and went around the block and came back in the side door. He told his uncle that Coble was pretty mad and talked about a big showdown on the media or else moving away and leaving the mess. They had a good laugh. Ray said, "We'll let him stew about it. Maybe I should go over and get him riled up worse, and then later ask him over for some barbecue. We'll hold you back for a while and spring it on him."

"I don't think you need to rile him up any more. I think

he'll do a pretty good job on himself. Might give it away if you went over there."

"Yeah. I know. I just like to hear him get going on the Constitution again, is all."

Ray gave him a tour of the city and Friday night they went out to his music hangout and had a good time. Howard expressed his enthusiasm for Texas by drinking a lot of pitcher beer. He remembered coming back late and seeing Coble's place dark, the moonlight shining on his bay of wreckage, pieces floating there like the aftermath of a hurricane.

Early Saturday morning he woke on the couch to the grinding squeal of a winch dragging a steel cable straight through his hangover. He went back to sleep and woke up a few times, aware of a commotion but not about to get up, until he heard men talking and unloading a Bobcat and he had to see what was happening.

He pulled back the curtain on the side window. Next door there was a battered one-ton dump truck from Pete's Recycling sitting in the backyard with an old six-wheel lowboy trailer. The bucket of the Bobcat was about to engage a doorless refrigerator half buried by the garage, and a tilt-bed tow truck from Bayou Towing was winching the hulk of a rusted Pontiac clear of the heavy weeds under a magnolia tree. He woke his uncle.

Ray couldn't believe it. He said, "I think he made us. I

think he's doing this to make me feel like a rat. I know he's not afraid of the city. He loves taking on the system. He's getting me back. I'd bet on it. Let's wait and see if he comes over."

It went on all day. By sundown the last car was loaded up, the appliances were gone, and they had begun picking up the small stuff and throwing it on the truck. Ray started thinking he should go over there, that it looked worse for him to pretend he didn't know what was going on. On the other hand, Coble might have put two and two together and cleaned the yard to spite him, or he might have figured that the no-account northerner had actually put the law on him. He figured he could get a hostile reception if he went over there.

So Howard laid low for his entire two-week job search, never using the front door but always going in the side door to the lower level and driving around the block so as not to drive by the Coble place, and after a few interviews and without finding a job to his liking he drove back to Minnesota. He called a week later and Uncle Ray said he still couldn't figure out what to do. The longer he stayed away the more it would look like he set the fake inspector up, and he was starting to think it was a dead giveaway. On the other side, if Coble was mad then the longer the wait the more time there was for him to cool off.

He said he was in a bind. How could he not go over, after all the work the man did to clean up his yard; he wished he'd gone over there right away. And if Coble knew it was a setup at least they could have had a laugh about it and he could have smoothed it over with a little whiskey. But he had become caught in limbo. He figured Coble was sticking it to him, because why didn't he come over himself and talk about his big cleanup project?

So he sat in an odd state of paralysis; couldn't figure if the man was mad at him or pulling a scam right back at him. He said he may have underestimated the level of talent down there.

The next week Howie called again. Ray said he finally went over there with a bottle of bourbon. He said Coble was smiling. Coble said, "What took you so long? I've been expecting you for weeks."

"You figured it out, huh?"

"I knew you sent that guy right from the get-go. I knew it when he walked up the drive. Before he knocked on the door, I knew."

"You did? How'd you know that?"

"Well for one thing, you know they don't just go walking around doing that stuff here, and he didn't hold out any ID or anything, and I didn't see any city car out there. And he talked just like you do. But I didn't need any of that. I knew before he hit the door, and you want to know how I knew? You want the dead giveaway?"

"Well, yeah."

"He was wearing my suit. The guy was wearing my own suit." He grinned wider.

"Your suit?"

"You don't remember, do you? Years ago, when you had to go to the wedding for that guy at work and you borrowed that suit from me?"

"Oh jeez. That's right. Oh man. Oh, for dumb."

"That's right. Dumb is a good word, Ray."

"And I never brought it back . . ."

"I told you to keep it. It was already too small for me, even back then." Then he lowered his voice and put his hand on Ray's shoulder and got close and serious. Looked him straight in the eyes: "But Ray, y'know, if you're gonna play a joke, I mean, fine, I'm down for that. I like jokes. I really do. But don't send in some guy wearing my own suit. You gotta do better than that. I mean seriously, man. You insulted me. That bothers me. I'm actually hurt, that you would think so little of me. Like I'm stupid. That you would think I'd be so easy, like I was just some schoolboy chump. Like I was born yesterday . . ." He paused, took a deep breath, and then said, "I've been around, Ray. You gotta show a little bit of respect, y'know? Man to man?" His face was terribly serious, as if he might even cry.

Ray felt miserable, he said—"lower than whale shit and

that's on the bottom of the ocean"—and he got this glum look himself and began to fumble out an apology, "Dammit, Hank . . . I'm sorry . . . you're right . . . that was pretty dumb . . ." and when he finished Coble broke into loud whoops of laughter. Laughed until he was sore, Ray said, and pretty soon he started to laugh himself.

12

ATTITUDE

BACKING INTO THE ALLEY BEHIND THE Fitzgerald Theater in St. Paul—or just about any city alley—is showtime for a trucker. The one at the Fitz is trickier than most because it's not at ninety degrees to the street. It angles away on the blind side, and the truck can only get at it by coming down the right lane of the one-way and swinging hard left into a small parking lot across the street from it. A stagehand has to come out and stop traffic while I ease back, guessing at the angle as the trailer squeezes past that corner on the right side. I can't see the dock until the tractor clears the lot and gets cranked straight with the trailer.

It usually draws a small audience of those waiting to get by. I did it cleanly that time and they stood in awe, and some smiled and waved. When I mess it up and have to jack back and forth a few times they leave with eyes down, embarrassed for me.

Leaving that acute-angled alley there's no way to make a right turn onto the one-way so I need another stagehand to stand fearless in the face of oncoming traffic, holding them at the corner while I hog the street and head right at them. Most understand the situation but there's usually at least one who honks, either in fear or from righteous outrage. I swung wide left onto Seventh for two blocks, another left and up the hill, timed the lights to hit the downhill ramp in seventh gear, and wound 'er up onto eastbound I–94, heading for Kentucky.

· · ·

Lexington is a most agreeable city. That Friday, November 10, I went to a Thoroughbred auction in an auditorium complex built for the purpose. Big trees, shady grounds, fine old buildings, everything kept in good order. I found the semicircular steep-sloped auction ring and sat in close. The racing business took on an unexpected grandeur when the first horse strutted into the circle and about knocked me over just from his sheer shining presence. Grace, strength, tone, sheen, attitude; I'd never seen so much of it all in one place. He looked good, he knew he looked good, he could tell *we* knew he looked good. And of course looking good wasn't even what this was all about. This was all about blinding speed, speed and attitude. The essentials.

People who spend their time around animals this powerful tend to move deliberately and talk slow and soft. A person can feel his own thin-skinned frailty compared to all that toned muscle, those hard hooves, that gorgeous hide, that thick mane and those big blunt teeth; this is a huge athlete all wired up, nearly quivering to break into a gallop. I wondered what was going on behind the soft eyes and had no idea what he might have been thinking. I figured he was smart in a language I'd never understand.

There were more stunning creatures presented that afternoon than in a Miss Universe showdown. The auctioneers kept a running singsong in the air and money flew at the slightest nod, sometimes in five figures but most often in six, and a few times in seven. At the first million-dollar horse I wouldn't admit to being flabbergasted but I will say I was real impressed. It was about as close to flabbergast as I need to get. The atmosphere, the money, the stables, the rhythm of the auctioneers, the buyers, the handlers, the setup, and especially the horses. High excitement in a low-key setting.

Took the rig back to Minnesota after the load out Saturday night. We had the next week off and on Wednesday, November 22, I slipped out of the city just after one o'clock, heading for New York again. Made the first Chicago outskirts around eight, sailed by the Loop at nine thirty, caught the Indiana Tollway and ended up in a motel in Goshen. They said on the phone it was only a couple miles off the tollway but it was twelve; I was there only because I remembered the 800 number of the motel chain.

Woke up to a gray morning, about fifteen degrees out. Started the truck and left it running, suddenly realizing that ten years ago if you left a truck shut off in fifteen degree weather you would need professional help to get started in the morning. Things have progressed all around us, most of the time with nobody even commenting on it.

I walked a block to an odd cafe, a square room of tables with booths on the sides and no counter; wolfed the three-egg special with the corned beef hash, drank most of the pot of coffee, read the election news, and by midafternoon I had slogged through Ohio for about the seventieth time and was sailing into sweet Pennsylvania. Except this time it wasn't so sweet. A swirling snow made the Appalachians a long crawl; there were two truck wrecks on the westbound side, flashing red and blue lights spearing through the snowfall in the early dark. I spent hours without getting into high gear.

The weather cleared and the road dried somewhere around Milton and what a good feeling that was, and night fell, and fifty miles later I settled into a good rhythm and then at seventy miles an hour I hit a solid whiteout in the Pocono Mountains. I backed all the way down into seventh gear and then into sixth, twenty miles an hour, switched on the road lights and the Jake Brake and locked the differential, the engine holding back on long curving downgrades with the lights barely revealing the first dozen feet beyond the hood; all the time I was hoping not to get hit from behind by one of winter's optimists. Strained for the guidance of the right edge of the road and was grateful for the rumble strips on the shoulder, the snow a blinding swirl of white pyrotechnics erupting out of the black, from below and above and all around. It was like a sustained two-hour video game with static and I focused on nothing but staying on the pavement and squinting to see that no one was sitting crosswise in the darkness ahead.

I ground on past a couple of small wrecks, flashing lights of patrol cars cutting into the night, to storm relief at Stroudsburg, near the Delaware Water Gap and the Jersey line. The truck stop used to be a homey little place until it one day morphed into a brightly lit shopping maze with bad food. The Professional Drivers Only section was nearly empty except for three young hustlers in baggy pants who didn't look anything like truck drivers, or even like future truck drivers. It took the waitress a while to make her appearance.

"Coffee, and the twelve-ounce T-bone," I said.

"Don't have no twelve-ounce T-bone," she said.

"You got any kind of T-bone?"

"No; sure don't."

"It's on the menu."

"I know it. But we don't serve it no more."

"Got any steak at all?"

"Nope."

"I guess I'll have the meat loaf then."

"We're outa meat loaf."

"Uh-huh. Well, then, I'll go with the beef stew."

"Outa that, too."

"Got any chicken, the dark meat?"

"All outa chicken. We did have it but it's gone."

"Huh. How about the fish?"

"Yeah, we got that."

"Okay."

"What kinda dressin' on the salad?"

"Thousand Island."

"We don't have that."

"For chrissakes."

"We got ranch, blue cheese, French—"

"Gimme the blue cheese."

"What kinda potatoes? We got hash browns—"

"French fries." She left and I didn't see her for a while and I knew the fish would be lousy and so would the fries. But from there the motel was only a block away and they had a small lounge, and New York was just a short run in the morning, and the day could have ended a whole lot worse.

We loaded into the Town Hall in Manhattan the next morning and I left the rig at a Penske truck lot behind a refinery in Linden, New Jersey, called a taxi, and flew home for a month. We leave the truck there when they've got room, which they generally don't. Went back on Friday, December 22, and my cabdriver was from the old school: heavyset guy in a big old Chevy station wagon with the big engine, lots of torque, bad shock absorbers, no cruise control. He slouched back behind the wheel at an angle, half resting against the door, the easier to turn around and talk; his right foot stabbed the accelerator in a persistent slow rhythm and the wagon lurched and bounded with every beat. Rrrrrm-rrrrrm-rrrrrm-rrrrrm, rocking like a fishing boat in the waves. At first I thought he just liked to feel the power but we got in steady traffic at fifty and he still kept that same beat so it must have been something deeper, some bedrock planetary throbbing felt by only a few souls in touch with subsurface extra-long wavelengths. I figured he must be getting about four miles to a gallon, goosing it every three seconds like that.

He talked about snow in Buffalo, and about the Giants and the Knicks and how Jersey had the most restrictive pollution laws in the country and that's why all these buildings were standing empty; no commercial property around there had changed hands in the last six years. Place is fallin' apart, he said; nobody can afford the cleanup. "Looka that; broken glass, roof fallin' in. It'd cost ten times what it's worth to dig it all out and fill it back in. So there it sits, for years. Empty. Go figure."

The truck started on the first try, after sitting all those weeks, and the Jersey Turnpike was right around the corner. Heading north through all the industry I saw the famous skyline across the Hudson to the right: offices and stores over there, dock cranes and catalytic towers here.

Manhattan is a simple town to a highway truck. City trucks have a lot of bridges and tunnels to choose from, but with a tall semi it just about has to be the George Washington Bridge, and from there you go down either Broadway or Second Avenue. That's it. Grand Forks, North Dakota, gives you more options than that. I took my usual Broadway route, got on at 178th Street and then at 65th, Lincoln Center, angled off down on Ninth Avenue to 57th; traffic moved aside and made room and I turned right to Eleventh and left down to 33rd Street by the Convention Center. There are four blocks set aside there, curb parking on both sides, for show trucks to wait; it's amazing. I snagged a taxi to the hotel, got another on Saturday when it was time to load out, and it couldn't have been simpler.

It could have been faster, though, because it takes forever to drive 150 blocks in that Saturday-night traffic. Which is why truckers wince when you say *New York*.

Best to just relax and enjoy the show, the streets full of action, the hyperactive traffic.

The trip out there in November had been through snow and ice and sudden whiteouts in the Appalachians and in the Poconos, but coming back on Christmas Eve day the sun was out and traffic was light. A little snow in western Pennsylvania, not so bad. There had been a couple of big storms the previous week. By Christmas Day the roads were dry, but in the snow-filled ditches and medians you could see the residue of scores of ruined holidays, from the Allegheny River all the way to the St. Croix. Saw seven truck wrecks and too many cars to count.

Now, the millennium didn't end at the end of 1999. That was another terrific thing about the big changeover: It was so big we got to celebrate it twice. The millennium ended at the end of the year 2000, and it would have to be that way, because the first year wasn't zero, it was the year 1. So the first hundred years had to end at the end of A.D. 100, not at the end of A.D. 99.

On New Year's Eve of the real end of the twentieth century I was invited to be the sound man—kind of a misnomer there, in a lot of cases, not unlike the term *stable boy*—and sit in on electric guitar with my old band

Scooter Trash. We played a little place in a southern metro suburb. It had a center room with a U-shaped bar, a front room with games and sports, and a back dining room with a small quarter-circle stage in one corner. The back room was packed by the last set and we did a little countdown to midnight but didn't play "Auld Lang Syne" like blues bands usually don't, and nobody cared. They broke out bottles of cheap champagne and little plastic glasses and we did a Chicago shuffle and a Jimmy Reed spread and a slow blues and the dance floor got crowded, which meant there were maybe nine or ten couples on it. A guy spilled a beer out there and it got slippery and nobody cared about that either.

We did a couple of encores but the lady manager was overly crabby, especially for such a momentous historical event, and she wanted us out, *out*, right away, and we wrapped it up and packed it up and she paid us and nagged us again and our harmonica player called her the *B* word and slammed the door and we all went our separate directions.

13

GERONIMO AND
ROBERT W. SERVICE

NEXT MORNING IT WAS JANUARY 2001. THE first month of the new thousand years, this time the real one, and still it was just another plain old January. On the first Monday morning I took the pickup to the cafe in New Richmond, speculated with a guy at the counter on whether the freezing rain would change into snow—which it was already doing, you could see it out the window. I headed east from there into unfamiliar territory in an attempt to get lost. It began snowing a little denser, soft flakes floating lightly and straight down, the sky flat and impassive, especially about the location of the sun.

A few miles out I turned north onto a trackless plain of virgin snow; a pure and slightly rounded surface, heading north to a gentle ridge a couple of miles off. The road was a large-diameter paper towel roll rising from an all-white snowscape; all bleached, all soft, all muted. I split the difference between two fence lines stringing the whiteness, keeping right down the middle of the mound.

In a farm corral off to the left were seven horses, some

wearing sporty blue warm-up blankets and some not. Five stood in profile against the blank background like cutouts but without shadows. Two were playing tag, making sudden cuts and moves, rubbing the sides of their heads together, or their necks, each trying to corner the other.

After that it became a moody road, nothing moving, nothing new, all old, all run down. Barns stood in peeling white, farms slipped away in tangled fence wire and fallen sheds. Wooden hayracks listed to the side; crumbling stone foundations marked barns torn off by long-ago storms.

At an intersection a green metal sign leaned out of a snowbank, marking 170th Street and 220th Avenue. Except for the snow, it was the only new thing in sight. The horizon was a dark umber forest, shaded from gray to deep brown to black at the scalp line, sometimes a mile off, sometimes a quarter, sometimes next to the road; but always of deep woods, oak and maple and spruce, thick with undergrowth. It sat brooding still as carpet. Within its spreading miles creatures moved like mites.

There was in fact a lot going on in the frozen silence. The falling snow masked a thermonuclear ball throwing heat across ninety-three million miles of vacuum; the forest and farmhouses held multitudes of mammals, from voles to deer to bears, along with billions of hibernating insects. Farther along the road and beneath a ten-acre flat slab of whiteness lay ice, and below that a lake of thousands of fish; tails and fins rippling gently, hanging in the dark water. Beneath the hood of the pickup six thousand muffled explosions per minute moved the observer smoothly through the cold silence. Two hundred years ago, barely a wink of time, no one could have imagined luxury such as this, available these days to any working person: to cruise easily through a frozen land, warm and unhindered.

I had a camera. Everywhere I stopped to shoot, five more scenes jumped up; fences, tree lines, forlorn structures. A farm sat a quarter mile off between ridgelines, barely visible through the falling snow, floating mistily in there like a ship at sea. Near an intersection stood the fractured tower and twisted vanes of a wooden windmill, frosted like a strange cake. I wandered until the film ran out.

And about then I arrived at County K, took a left, and suddenly the snow quit, the sky brightened, and the sun broke through. The whole wonderful somber mood was ruined in less than five miles. There were abrupt shadows. When I hit the state highway they had already salted the surface. Oncoming traffic with headlights on threw salt slush at me. It's not surprising that people move to Alaska, I thought.

Commander Cody and His Lost Planet Airmen were on our stage in January 2001, part of a short reunion tour, which caused me to dig out my twenty-nine-year-old LP of *Hot Licks, Cold Steel & Truckers' Favorites* and to get Andy Stein and Bill Kirchen to sign it. There were reasons this was an all-time favorite trucker band and the song titles tell why: "Lookin' at the World through a Windshield," "Truck Drivin' Man," "Truck Stop Rock," "Semi-Truck," and the tear-jerker "Mama Hated Diesels." All those and "Kentucky Hills of Tennessee," "Rip It Up," "Watch My .38," "Diggy Liggy Lo," and "It Should've Been Me," plus the longnose Peterbilt on the cover and the cool old trucks on the back, make this album about as good as albums ever got. Class like this is hard to find in the music business these days. They jist don't make 'em like this'n no more.

At a party the next weekend the subject of winter came up, and of course how could it not, we being who we are. A carpenter named Mike who had worked on a fishing boat in Alaska, which was how he'd met the host of the party, told about a time when he drove down to the Chiricahua wilderness area in southern Arizona, in the Coronado National Forest. This was way back when he was single. It was March and he was sick of winter and he figured it would be warm down there, that close to the Mexican border. He had enough food for ten days and he meant to pack up into the mountains for a week of solitude. He got a Forest Service map, parked the car, and began hiking in. Spent the first night in the foothills on the western slope and woke up at four in the morning in a tent covered with snow. It was still coming down.

He thought he could hike above it, or that it would probably stop on its own soon. By daylight it was more than a foot deep. He began climbing, trying to follow the trail under the snow, and was quickly soaking wet. His gear was the old stuff, cotton and wool, and it wasn't waterproof and he was soaked right through the socks. It was getting colder and he figured the worst thing you can do up there in the mountains is to get wet. By midmorning he was nearly exhausted and he was eating up rations at a terrific rate to keep his body temperature up. He was about eight or nine miles into the high country by then.

He changed his plan. If he stayed up there another night he could freeze to death, so he figured to hell with the trails, they wound around too much, and what he needed to was to get back down to the desert floor as quickly as he could. He headed straight east out of the mountains, walking fast, and by noon had reached a point where a huge valley opened before him.

It was white as far as he could see. Snow completely covered the desert. Off in the distance he saw a small object, a man-made structure of some sort. Maybe a military installation. He would head for that; it was the only sign of humans all the way to the horizon. Beneath where he stood was a nearly vertical escarpment, a drop of about fifteen hundred feet. He wasn't a climber and had no gear for it, but he found a tight crevasse that descended between rock faces. Once on this path, which he couldn't see in its entirety, there was no climbing back out; he didn't know if it would end in a sheer drop of eight hundred feet straight down or not, but he was sure he couldn't go back the way he came and make the floor by nightfall. And he didn't think he'd survive on the mountain in the light clothes he had. So he headed down among the sparse vegetation clinging to the rock, between the boulders jammed in the crack.

It was a frightening descent. If he lost his grip along the way and began to slide he would surely accelerate and fall off a precipice; he wondered what that might be like, to spend your last few seconds falling through the air in such a beautiful place. Plenty have done it, he thought. It held to its jagged narrow shape and when he finally found the rocky bottom he sat for a minute and then began his trek to the rectangular object, thankful to be on a horizontal plane.

It looked at first like it might be three to five miles away, but he walked for two hours and it seemed to get bigger but not closer. When he finally got near he saw a broad smooth path heading off in both directions and felt a hard surface under the snow—US 80, between Douglas and Lordsburg. He crossed to the structure, which he had been assuming to be a mine head or a missile silo or some strange weather station, except now it was looking very much like a monument. He brushed off a bronze plate. It said that on this spot in 1890 or thereabouts Geronimo had surrendered to Captain So-and-so and by that action officially ended the armed conflict between the United States and the native peoples. (I checked later; it was in 1886 and he surrendered to General Nelson Miles.)

He went back to the road. He wasn't going to leave this place; there wasn't a sign of any other construction as far as could be seen, and the afternoon was fast slipping away. He had eaten most of his rations. His clothes were still soaking wet and it was getting colder. There were no tracks on the highway, meaning not one vehicle had passed since the snow had fallen that morning. After an hour or so something square hove into sight from the south, an RV. He stood on the road and waved as it approached, an older couple clearly visible through the big windshield. As they drove by he saw her reach up and push down the lock on her door.

He stood and watched them disappear toward Lordsburg. To New Mexico. The name sounded like heat. He thought of a warm cafe, a dark saloon, a shot of whiskey, a motel bed. He watched the roof disappear in the cloud of virgin snow that followed it. He wondered if they thought anything about abandoning a man in a cold desert as night was falling. He said, "Did they wonder how I'd come to be standing in the middle of a snow-covered desert? Do you think they gave a damn? Did they think they just had a close call with a jail breaker?"

He hopped around to keep warm. Did some push-ups. Dug through his pack for an extra shirt. And just before it got dark a black dot of hope emerged from the bleakness to the south. At first he thought it might be some kind of reverse mirage, but it was clearly getting larger. He stood directly in the center of the road and waved both arms over his head in big semicircle motions like the old navy drill. As it sharpened into view he saw it was a 1949 Ford pickup, black and battered, and although it was moving slow, maybe twenty miles an hour, it didn't move any slower as it came up to him and he could see the face of the driver inside. He said, "You know how sometimes you see somebody and their face is so wild and they look so out there you just know immediately that this person is not here, this guy is way off somewhere else? That man-from-Mars skid-row kind of look? I mean, they aren't just dirty and down and out, but there's that wild look to their eyes? I could see that through the windshield; it looked like pure evil. I don't scare easy but this guy was scary. I jumped out of the way and quit waving and I just stood there and watched him go by. I was glad, too. I thought to myself, I'm just lucky that son of a bitch didn't stop."

He stood watching as the pickup chugged on to the north. It was about half a mile away when he heard it squeak to a stop and then the clashing of gears as the driver found reverse and then the laboring *rrrirwr-rrirwr-rrirwr-rrirwr-rrirwr* as it backed up. He watched it approach with as much melancholy as relief. At least something is going to change, he thought, but it might not be for the better. When the truck finally ground to a halt he could see it had been painted with a brush, layer upon cracked layer of black paint, like an old locomotive. He opened the passenger door and the man croaked: "Throw yer bag in the back." He moved to toss the pack over the side and saw a headless bloody torso split wide open end to end, lying there on its back amid the loose metal and chains and burlap bags; the floor of the bed was awash in drying blood.

He recoiled and then realized it was an eviscerated hog.

He tried to push the pack up against a hairy part of the back to keep it away from the deepest liquid. He got in the truck. The man had long stringy gray hair and a long uneven beard and his face was deeply crisscrossed with cracks, thin embedded furrows of black grease and dirt. The eyes were mobile, sometimes narrowed down to slits in the fractured facescape but mostly opened out so that you could see more white than a person is comfortable seeing. He didn't respond to nervous small talk. Mike said, "I had my hand on that door handle the whole time—I saw he had a big butcher knife in a sheath on his leg. It had short little hog hairs around the handle and it was smeared with blood, and there was blood on the sheath and on his old pants. I kept trying to start some kind of conversation, like how strange the weather was and when was the last time anybody's seen snow on this desert, and he wouldn't say anything. I had no idea what was going through his mind but I figured it probably wasn't good.

"Then suddenly he turned and he grabbed my left arm, really tight, and man he had strong hands, like eagle talons, like a damn death grip, and he looked at me with those weird eyes and he said: 'I am the fifth person to live in this body.' Man, I was just about ready to bail right there, except where in the hell was I going to go? So I said something kind of noncommittal, like oh really or something, and he started to talk."

He talked and talked. He said every time he drove by that monument the spirit of Geronimo would come down on him and give him a bad time and he'd argue and he and Geronimo would fight like hell, not really fight but shout and holler at each other. He said he thought Mike was Geronimo and that's why he came back for him.

"Well, I hate to disappoint you, but I'm not Geronimo."

"How do you know?"

"Well, I'd know. I didn't grow up around here, for one thing."

"You don't know that. You only think that. You could be Geronimo and you don't think so right now but he could come out any minute and you'd find out the truth. He's probably been living in your body since you were a little shit."

"Um, I suppose. But I don't think I'm Geronimo anyway."

"Then why were you at the monument? Why were you there?"

"I came out of the mountains. I was going camping and it snowed and I had to come down where it was warmer. I wasn't dressed for it."

"That's just what you think. You don't think if Geronimo was living in your body he wouldn't want to come back to this place? You ever think about that?"

"No, I didn't."

"You'd never climb down those mountains on this side if you didn't want to come to the monument, 'cause there ain't one goddamn other thing here. You wouldn't be here if Geronimo didn't want you to be here, 'cause that's jist the way it is."

He quit fighting the idea. He asked the man what he was going to do with the hog. He said he was taking it to a butcher in Lordsburg and selling it. He also had a couple of cases of cigarettes he had bought in Mexico that he was selling to a guy he knew. He said the Border Patrol all knew him and they never bothered him when he came across from Mexico with cigarettes.

You raise hogs, do you? Mike asked him. He said no, he was a handyman kind of guy, fixed cars and did a little welding, had an old torch and a couple of tanks he'd found. He said the hippies who lived on the back side of the hill from him had pigs and traded him the hog for fixing their old bus. He talked the whole rest of the way to Lordsburg but Mike kept his grip on the door handle all the same. He said, "I never knew when he might get going and fly off and try to kill me because I was Geronimo. I got out in kinda the center of town and walked to a motel and then I went to a bar and had a shot and a burger and started talking to some people, and I said I needed to go up to the park to get my car and three women there were going up there the next day."

So what were the women like? "Well, actually that turned into a whole 'nother story. But I'll tellya later." He may have meant that he had told a long enough story already and he may have meant he didn't want to go into it with his wife sitting there.

. . .

Our show went to Europe again, to Berlin and Dublin, but this time they were able to get along without their truck driver. Sitting at home I recalled the big storm that hit the country eight years ago at that same time, March 1993. It could have been perfect and it may have been not quite perfect, but it was close enough that we got buried in Alabama. Zero degrees and snowdrifts up to your belt buckle; we expected to do a show in warm sunny Birmingham but it felt like Bemidji, the very thing we tried to escape. The blizzard moved in Friday morning, as we were loading into the Alabama Theatre, and we ended up frozen into downtown that night. I recalled Robert W. Service and that line from "The Shooting of Dan McGrew," talking of the cold through the parka's fold, stabbing like a driven nail.

The red-and-blue neon sign in the window of the pool hall across the snowbound street from our hotel looked like a beacon of hope in a bitter frozen wilderness:

warmth and sanctuary against nature gone berserk, and all that business. Five or six of us slogged over there and had hot dogs for dinner at the bar, and at that point hot dogs were good enough. The word *hot* was good enough. We were grateful the electricity was still on. Service had written about the miner dog dirty and loaded for bear, stumbling from out of the night, which was fifty below, and into the din and the glare. It felt like that.

There was also a fight in there that night, perhaps driven by the hostile weather or the fact that most of Birmingham's finest were off preoccupied with the blizzard. We never heard what ignited it, but it would not have been out of place in the Dan McGrew context. There were a couple of young ladies standing by and it was a competitive event, the pool shooting was, and two young men were suddenly flaring at each other like banty roosters. At that point in the poem the miner was saying something like, I want to state, and my words are straight, and I'll bet my gold they're true; that one of you is a Hound of Hell, and that one is Dan McGrew.

One of our combatants suggested that the other's mother walked on four legs and the other responded with a vulgar reference to the first's entire family, and the first challenged the second to repeat that observation, which of course he did, and there followed a brief but vigorous tussle in which a few awkward but enthusiastic punches landed, before spectators jumped in and brought it under control. Nothing as vivid as Service's ending, where McGrew ends up pitched on his head and pumped full of lead and the miner dies in the arms of his love, the Lady That's Known As Lou, as she simultaneously slips his gold into her purse.

But the event stirred our interest to the point that we actually ordered a second glass of beer, thinking we might see another free sporting event. It was a sparkling finish to a dramatic day. When we had pulled into town Thursday it was warm, the sun was shining, everything green and peaceful. No sign of snow, no hint of animosity.

There is a singular lack of snow machinery in Alabama—a dearth of plows—which is of course why people from here move there. Saturday the broad assumption in town was that our show would be canceled: no buses, no taxis, almost nothing moving at all, houses and stores buttoned up under great drifts. Precious few local crew members showed up for work at the hall. One who did asked if we brought the weather with us. Emmylou Harris and her band made it down from Nashville in a custom bus, incredibly, and as showtime approached I took the truck out and around the city to track down our guest gospel quartet, the Birmingham Sunlights.

It was our last year in a straight truck and it was a good thing we had it there; the big rigs just aren't cut out for rescue work. No traffic anywhere and I tore hell-bent across a long four-lane bridge, over railroad yards and a river, and at the center of the span the left duals somehow straddled a steel rail, unseen under all the snow, and it threw the truck into a spectacular spin, a full 360-degree circle, and it ended up facing the right way without losing too much time in the process. I had a city map and the addresses and once the first of the Sunlights came aboard there was a guide as well, and off we went for the others; I only needed to fetch three because one had made it in on his own. Heading into a nice wooded suburb we came down a shallow hill and at the bottom a good-sized tree lay all across the road, but it was the top of the tree, not the main trunk, and it was apparent that if we stopped and backed and went the long way around we'd never get to the show in time. With nothing to lose I laid on the coal and we tore through the crown of that tree like it was a tumbleweed.

The second singer was in a bind. His wife was with child and ready to deliver any moment and he couldn't leave her there alone. We brought them all aboard and they took it pretty well, considering they faced the possibility of having a child delivered in a snowbank by two singers and a truck driver, and off we went for the third man. He lived out where the phone lines were down and was taken by surprise when we showed up at his door. He got his stage clothes together and we set off, four guys and a woman and a child about to make its appearance to the world, six souls crammed into a truck cab designed for two. Changing gears with that long floor shift was a real delicate exercise in respecting personal boundaries.

We blasted back into the city and went scrambling into the stage door fifteen minutes before sign-off, just in time for them to get on the air. They did one tune and then everyone got together for the big closing number, and then, off air, they treated our tiny brave audience to one of the most remarkable encores in show business history, considering. We heard that the baby arrived two days later, a girl.

We were so short on help we had to get a volunteer from the audience to run the spotlight, and in an audience that small we hated to lose even one. I wished later that in doing the credits at the end we could have named everyone in the audience as well; it wouldn't have taken much longer.

The wild weather wasn't over, either; on May 7 of that year there was a huge tornado outbreak across the country, with touchdowns from Texas to the Canadian border. Someday old-timers will talk about '93.

14
TWO SHOTS

IT WAS AN EASY WINTER, ALL THOSE shows at home in January and February. When they came back from Europe we did a quick little run down to Purdue University in Lafayette, Indiana, and then had four more weeks in the Fitzgerald Theater in St. Paul.

I went out to scour the outlying acreage for useful detail. Some small towns have coffee shops now, so they'll have two breakfast places, one serving up ordinary coffee and bacon and eggs and the other offering flavorful coffees and European pastries. One full of young and old stocky guys in work clothes and caps and the other half-full of people who don't look like they are dressed to lift much weight at all; and it appears that neither group is much missing the presence of the other.

In a small town north of the cities on March 6th I found myself naturally in the heavy lifting cafe, preferring its noisy high-protein ambience to the genteel low-fat quiet of the coffee shop. The waitress was a tanned and feisty woman named Maria, sort of a healthier-looking and trimmer Roseanne Barr, who ran the place like a cheerful straw boss. When she took your order she put it in such a way as if you were following her order ("Now you're probably gonna want our homemade sausage with that, arencha"), which seemed to suit just about everyone, especially early in the morning. I sat at the counter and an older cowboy type sat down at the end, on the short leg of the L; he was wearing a black and beaten western hat with an irregular sagging brim and a flat crown, and a solid blue kerchief inside his jacket collar.

During a lull in the action Maria stopped by the counter and the cowboy guy said, "So how's your love life these days?"

"Aaah, good. Can't complain."

"Still havin' fun?"

"Yah. No problems."

"And how about your son? He doin' okay too?"

"Well, I got a little ticked off at him the other day. Y'know, somethin' in these kids nowadays; I dunno."

"What happened?"

"Well, this guy came in here and told me about this Ambrose fella, I forget his last name, a farmer south of here, he had a pole barn with five thousand bales of hay he wanted to get rid of. A buck a bale. Gave me his phone number and directions. So I called Ricky and told him to take the pickup and get his ass down there and buy a hundred bales. He says he's got his fish house in the pickup and I say okay, you don't need to bring any of it back, just go give the guy a check for a hundred bucks and tell'im we'll come and get it Saturday."

"And Ricky—does what?"

"I tell him twice; I say, look, somebody is gonna come in there and buy the whole five thousand bales and haul 'em all away somewhere and sell 'em for two dollars a bale, so you gotta get down there right away. And in the meantime I call Ambrose and get the answering machine and I leave a message that we're comin' in and we want a hundred bales, and hold 'em for us and Ricky'll be there with a check. And the next morning I call to say I'm comin' to start haulin' my hundred bales, and you guessed it."

"All gone."

"Yep. A guy came in and bought the whole shebang. Ricky never showed up. Started unloading the fish house and then one thing led to another and he forgot. But I think he didn't forget at all, I think he just figured the hay would be there and I was bein' too paranoid about somebody buyin' it all, and he just didn't think it was that big a deal. So now I gotta buy a hundred bales somewhere else for a buck and a half, at least, which means I'm out fifty dollars, for sure. Maybe more. I ask the kid, for chrissakes, Ricky, how long you think I gotta work to make fifty dollars? And you just throw it away like that? Why in hell doncha think about somebody besides yourself now and then? I was pissed."

"What did he say?"

"Aah, he said he was sorry. . . you know that routine: Sorry, Mom. I said, sorry my big fat butt; *I'm* the one out the fifty bucks. But y'know, maybe he'll learn somethin' from it. Hell, I don't know. You do whatcha can, know what I mean? He's not a bad kid."

"No. He's a good kid. But they do seem to be less, I dunno, less serious about stuff like that, these days."

"Ya, for sure. Tell me about it. If I'da done something like that at his age I'da got my ass kicked from here to Hinckley and back." She grabbed menus and hustled off to clear a couple plates and take some orders.

Another man came and sat next to the cowboy on the last stool at the end of the short leg of the counter, a pleasant-looking deliberate gray-haired man with a mustache and a pipe, in a topcoat. Maria sat him a clear plastic glass of water and a menu and on her next trip by, the glass and water and ice cubes all went flying. She stopped and laughed and said, "What?! You got so excited to see me you knocked over your water!?! Haha!" She got the counter cleaned up, laughing all the while, having a great time with it, and I was left wondering what happened, even though it happened right in front of me. If she would have apologized I would have concluded she knocked the glass flying, but her jolly reaction made him look like the clumsy one.

It was a modest room crowded with folding tables and plain chairs, with a painted fake brick wainscot up to table height and a couple of windows on the main street. The floor and the formica counter were both worn in specific spots, from thirty years of chair legs and men's elbows. A tough-looking workman sat with a snapped leather holster strapped to his hip, worn and weathered from a lot of miles on the trail; looked like it might hold a small pistol, derringer size, but then I saw the short black antenna of a cell phone sticking out. Times have changed but we still need to carry stuff on our hip.

It had the feeling that if the finishes were upgraded they might lose the clientele. That there are a lot of people who are comfortable only in humble surroundings and a room with a high ceiling and big laminated wood beams, nice light fixtures and an unmarked floor looks like nothing but money to them, and they figure the only way the owner is going to pay for all that luxury is by screwing the customer on the price of breakfast.

Which reminded me of a bar in Anchorage, Alaska, and their T-shirt that reads: CHILKOOT CHARLIE'S—WHERE WE SCREW THE OTHER GUY AND PASS THE SAVINGS ON TO YOU.

On the main street on the way out a video store with a marquee advertised three current hits:

COMING SOON:

BLESS THE CHILD

BRING IT ON

BEDAZZLED

We took another spring tour in May 2001, to Norfolk, Virginia, and Laramie, Wyoming. Coming into Norfolk from the west on Interstate 64 I rolled for two hours through a thick forest of flowering trees, growing in the median and at the side, tight to the road. Dogwoods, small purple magnolias they call tulip trees, pear trees, and some trees with slim white leaves. Those heavy trees looked good close like that, no ditches, a zero-tolerance roadway for strengthening the gene pool by thinning out the easily distracted. They also give the pleasant delusion that the whole territory between the Blue Ridge Mountains and the Atlantic Ocean is mostly an uninhabited forest. There were exits, like Oilville, Goochland and Short Pump, and downtown Richmond, but it was mostly woods and at the end of it we sailed out over the big bay and then dived right into it, like a whale. Came up on the other side, dry. A wonderment.

It's the world's largest naval base, with the kind of raucous, crude history you'd expect from such a place, but it didn't feel that way. I took the walking tour and saw St. Paul's Episcopal Church, built in 1739 to replace the old Chapel of Ease from 1641. It held a cannonball embedded in its solid brick southeast wall. A stone plaque set in the wall beneath the cannonball, which is buried flush with the brick surface, said, FIRED BY LORD DUNMORE JAN 1, 1776. Someone in the group asked if he'd been trying to hit the plaque.

In the Civil War it was used as a chapel by Union forces, who trashed the place as if they were a rock band, a big one; after the war the government paid the congregation thirty-six hundred dollars for damages. It was also the site of the funeral of General Douglas MacArthur.

The battleship *Wisconsin* was moored right smack downtown, a force at Leyte Gulf, Luzon, Iwo Jima, Japan, Korea, and the Gulf War, with veterans who had heard her guns roar for real to show people around. The links on the anchor chain weighed 120 pounds apiece; the main guns threw shells heavier than a small car twenty-three miles with accuracy not obtainable in a target rifle, and they did it on the move. It is one of the loudest and most accurate sites on the Register of Historic Places.

The Great Dismal Swamp lay just to the south of there, 223,000 acres, a literary name if ever there was one. They said Laura Ingalls Wilder wrote about it. The reeds are so tall they make tunnels for your boat. They said it's haunted and there are snakes in the water. I didn't go out there. Didn't have the time, y'know.

We left Norfolk on a fine Sunday morning, the truck and I, cruising north through the older part of the city, through Ward's Corners, once called "The Times Square of the South." With the tallest building in the area topping out at three stories it's kind of a stretch, and given the swampy ground and the shortage of bedrock around Hampton Roads—and possibly for other reasons—the South ultimately decided that one Times Square was enough.

Stopped at White's at Steele's Corner, Virginia, a favorite truck stop, to revisit the immense Australian crocodile and the other macabre goodies there. The wild boars, the sizable gun and knife collection, the menacing fish and the Great White Shark—a dark gallery of interesting ways that your precious flesh could be torn asunder. In contrast to living on a live volcano, urging you to lead life recklessly, this display inspires a life of alertness and caution.

The talk that day was about the general ineptitude of the traveling public, as it often is in the Professional Drivers Only section of a truck stop. Various recent encounters with cars seemingly bent on self-destruction; a driver described an incident in Florida where some old geezer blew right through a stop sign in front of him and caused him to leave some serious rubber on the highway. These incidents are not amusing to truckers, especially when tires cost more than three hundred dollars apiece and we've got eighteen of them. A smiling robust-looking lady driver there asked the room in general "Y'all know who lives in Florida?" and when nobody knew she said, "Old people—and their parents."

Fueled up and headed south on I–81, bound for I–64 and the wide open spaces out west. Crossed the high pass over the New River Valley, looked out over miles of green West Virginia hills; hard to imagine a place so beautiful being a favorite butt of jokes.

In Kentucky (WELCOME TO KENTUCKY—EDUCATION PAYS) I eased down through flat outcroppings, driplets seeping through the limestone, working on making farmland for the next geologic epoch. Stopped overnight east of Lexington and got a good early start on Monday, cruising on west to the drama of the high delicate crossings of the Ohio River at Louisville.

Kentucky's gentle roll continued though southern Indiana, through the farmland and the unsung oil fields with the old pumpers lazily cranking up and down, unnoticed. Had breakfast at a town called Dale, as if they couldn't choose what kind of dale they wanted—River, Oak, Elm,

Pine, Spring, Rose, Lons, Mon, Chippen, Hillen, Annan, Brook—so they settled on plain old Dale.

Magnificent St. Louis came on with a quickening of the pace and a distant view of the Arch but I got taken by the sightseeing and nearly missed the hard right downtown exit to I–70, along the Mississippi shore. On the west side of the city there was a monster backup; been there for years. Three lanes funnel into one, and when I got into the single lane and looked over into the blocked-off part it looked drivable but abandoned. Finally got to the end of the faux construction and saw a pickup with yellow lights flashing on the roof and about four people in reflective highway gear, listlessly moving around. Hard to say what they were doing. I know it must have happened but I can't remember ever going through St. Louis without grinding along in third gear for an hour.

It was mostly flatland through Missouri and Kansas and all the way to central Colorado. Signs implored me to stop; that honest, it really is more interesting than a person might think: 16-INCH PORCELAIN DOLLS—FRESH FUDGE—TOFFEE—CAPS AND MUGS—SHOT GLASSES—OZARK LAND. STOP NOW. Then FIRST AMENDMENT ADULT BOOK STORE—NEXT EXIT—NO BOOTHS—NO SLEAZE. Near Emma, Missouri, I passed a semblance of a car, driven by an old man with his elderly lady, looking as if it had been assembled from many trips to the salvage yard. It was hung entirely with ornamental doodads, inside and out. There was so much there I couldn't focus on anything. The inside was crisscrossed with beads and small animals hanging in midair and odd amulets were stuck all over the outside. Maybe campaign buttons or badges, hard to say what they were, against all the faded colors of the car itself.

And after driving hundreds of miles of rough road I came upon a big construction site, and what were they putting money into but a couple of new weigh stations, one on either side; two more harassment stops in the never-ending bureaucratic gouging of truckers. It wasn't like I hadn't been checked five times already in the past two days. There's a reason so many seasoned drivers are getting the hell out and why the industry is pushing to have the age for commercial drivers licenses lowered to eighteen. Lots of trucking jobs available. Who in their right mind would want to be examined by the government, any government, two or three times every day?

And now that I'm worked up, is it possible even to imagine a less efficient way to collect taxes than at tollbooths? To bring all that tonnage to a halt, every day, all day long, stop it and start it? Waste all those tons of fuel and lose all those hours of work? They call it a user tax. Bullshit has never come down from any statehouse in a form more crystal pure than that. An old lady who can't even drive and never leaves her Park Avenue high-rise uses the toll roads every day, and so does everyone else. If you eat or wear clothes or live indoors you are using the roads. And we all know it.

· · ·

A sign near Abilene advertised the Greyhound Hall of Fame. Spent the night east of Salinas, got up later than I wanted to at 5:00 A.M. Left without breakfast and came upon signs for the CZECH MUSEUM AND OPERA HOUSE—YOU'LL LOVE IT. Then for WILSON—CZECH CAPITAL OF KANSAS. FESTIVAL—LAST SATURDAY IN JULY. Then came the GARDEN OF EDEN and the SMOKY HILL WINERY—WINE OUTLET—MADE FROM KANSAS GROWN GRAPES. The land began to break slightly into long low waves. Cattle grazed in the morning sun, the light directly on their glossy orange-red flanks, brilliant as wildflowers.

Surprised to see a couple of hundred miles more of oil fields through Kansas. Not all the pumps were in motion and I had to look to spot them. More roadside temptations: LIVE RATTLESNAKES—PET THE BABY PIGS—LIVE DONKEY—BUFFALO—PHEASANTS—QUAIL—RACCOONS—COYOTES—PEACOCKS—SEE THE LARGEST PRAIRIE DOG IN THE WORLD. And DON'T MISS THE HIGH PLAINS MUSEUM—AMERICA'S FIRST HELICOPTER. And the 1887 OPERA HOUSE.

I stopped at the Mitten Truck Stop in Oakley, Kansas, and had breakfast with a cowboy and driver called Caballo, who said he got the name not because he was good with horses but because he was big as a horse. He'd worked a million-acre ranch in New Mexico and told me secrets about training horses and breaking a fever, and he said horses like to play ball. You can buy a rubber Horse Ball at a good tack shop; it's big and has a loop on it. They'll pick it up and run with it; roll it, kick it. He thought highly of most horses and said they were smarter than they get credit for.

That afternoon I found myself in Wyoming in a wide pass at an elevation of 8,640 feet, more than half a mile higher than Denver. The highest point on Interstate 80, in fact. From the Laramie Range I saw the frosting line of the Snowy Range forty miles to the west, way up there at fourteen thousand feet, and down before me was a town lying loose in a wide spreading valley into which the double highways grandly curved. A car sailed by me bearing a bumper sticker: TWO WRONGS IS ONLY THE BEGINNING.

The snow in the ditch was a surprise, even knowing the altitude. The day before it was a sweltering ninety degrees in Kansas and I was cussing a malfunctioning air conditioner, and now here I was wondering how I could have climbed into snow without noticing it, without downshifting through steep cuts and up high mountain roads.

This wasn't a struggle. John McPhee's description of the big tilted plate that is the Great Plains came to mind, but it still seemed strange to be on flat ground that high in the air. There was a fourteen-hundred-foot drop to the floor of the valley and the road snaked through a construction zone to the exit, where a young woman in sunglasses directed traffic in the dust of bridge construction. It was fifty-six degrees down there and the wind was blowing something fierce.

There are similarities between Norfolk and Laramie. Military backgrounds, a lot of rowdy and downright murderous behavior in the early days, now settling into an atmosphere tolerant of boutiques and coffee shops. And the famous cannonball embedded in the wall of a Norfolk church, sent forth from a British ship in 1776, and its counterpart of two hundred years later, a rifle shot through the plate glass window of the Buckhorn Bar into the mirror on the beautiful back bar, just above head height. It's also a large hole, and also famous.

It was an easy load in, the show was good, the folks were terrific. Ended up sitting with the locals at the Buckhorn Saturday night, for the music. Had a good time there, without working at it.

I left Laramie on Sunday morning, the twentieth of May, and for some reason expected an easy drive. I was disabused of that goofy notion in less than two hours. North of Cheyenne at Chugwater it began to rain and a hard quartering headwind from the northwest chattered the windshield wipers on the glass. The truck couldn't pull into the heavy wind and I had to downshift. Off to the right Herefords stood in a draw in a parallel formation, their butts squarely to the wind and their ears forward. Looked like the wind was blowing right through. At Wheatland the horizontal cold rain crystallized into snow that piled up faster than the wipers could handle and I was surprised to be in a full-scale western blizzard. I flipped the air switch to lock the differential, putting power to the road with both drive axles and making the rig less eager to spin out. For most of the next hour I was fully engaged in the delicate art of staying between ditches. I was in a zone like Michael Jordan in a playoff game, thinking no mistakes and no turnovers. Especially no turnovers.

I exited to US 18 at Orin Junction, where the snow was letting up but the freezing wind tried to blow the truck off the parking lot. I ordered coffee and the Sunday Special, roast beef and gravy. A pipeline crew sat in the nearest booth, talking about the weather and how long before they'd be back out there. There was a family at one table and an older couple at another. The outside door opened and it was as if someone hit the PAUSE button; all conversation stopped. A stocky biker shuffled in, cold and stiff, his face bright red and everything else shiny wet black. He radiated cold. People across the room got cold. I looked out to the pumps and so did the crew and sure enough, there sat a black Harley. No windshield, no fairing. A shovelhead engine, so it was at least sixteen years old.

He asked the waitress how much a cup of coffee cost. In his situation I thought it strange he'd be concerned about the price. She said fifty cents and he said he'd have one. They asked where he was headed and he said Casper. One guy asked how much he would take for the motorcycle right now and when he smiled you could almost hear his face crack. Another guy offered to trade his '99 Suburban for it, and a third guy said, "You might be careful about that—his wife'll be comin' to Casper to track you down, 'cause it's her car."

He drank the coffee and paid for the fuel and was gone. It was thirty-four degrees outside and he had fifty-six miles to go, west, straight into the wind. The windchill on that bike had to be sixty below. The truck felt amazingly warm when I got back in, eastbound now and heading for Rapid City. Around Lost Springs the snow quit but the wind didn't and windmill blades were still whipping at high speed and flags were standing straight out as if starched and ironed. North of Lusk is plains country but still up at five thousand feet, and it warmed to fifty degrees and the sky began to break and about the time I saw the Black Hills the sun came out. Each rising of the prairie cast a long flat shadow on the next rise to the east. Seen from afar like that the hills are indeed black; they float above the plains on the northern horizon like legends. Which of course they are.

US 18 went to Mule Creek Junction, caught the southern part of the curves and valleys of the Hills and met 79, running north again to Rapid City. I fueled at the old Windmill Truck Stop and found a bargain motel up on the high ground by the freeway. Monday I finished the last six hundred miles on cruise control, sailing easily across South Dakota and southern Minnesota and back to the yard.

Something that most trucks have in common: They sound good when they start up and they sound even better when you shut 'em down.

15

CROSS COUNTRY

WE WERE HOME FOR A COUPLE OF WEEKS, a pause before the big spring tour, and in early June the state was hit with monster storms. News came from our friends in central Minnesota that on Monday the eleventh they had 65 miles per hour winds with a lot of rain, followed by more rain on Tuesday. A barn collapse killed twenty-six head of cattle on one farm. It took down all the trees in the yard of another farm up near Gilman, a place noted for its beautiful stand of evergreens; word got around and people from all over the county drove up to see it. I heard later those who went Thursday found a bare yard with a huge woodpile in the front and a bunch of chain saw guys sitting up on the top drinking beer. And what else could they do.

The ground was so wet nothing more could sink in. The rains were sitting there on the mud, waiting for space to be made down below in the aquifer or to be carried off in the air. Creeks were overflowing; no room in the swamp. Walking on the lawn was like walking on wet cake. Sullen gardeners sat in their kitchens, hands cupped around coffee turning cold while they went down their list of grievances against the spring of Aught One. Even those with flowers already up were saying, Well, sure, they're growing, but it's all foliage; the flowers are way behind, because it's too wet and too cool. Hardly any flowers on there at all.

Out in the fields the soybeans were in and up but needed hot weather to get growing and corn was in worse shape yet, with very little planted. Some had given up on planting corn at all that year. Others held to faint hopes, but it was not looking good.

It was still raining on Wednesday the thirteenth when my job took me mercifully out of earshot, as it often does, and I left for Memphis, leaving friends and neighbors to the misery of Minnesota weather. It may have made it worse for them that I was off to this particular city because I tend to run off about how much fun it is. Beale Street closed off, folks walking around carrying drinks— an impossibility in Minnesota—blues coming at you from all directions in all tempos, all day long. Ribs, gumbo, jambalaya, red beans and rice in the cafes. Sun shining on the street.

And all that music history in Sun Studio. The world changed in that studio, and you can go there and walk the very floors upon which it happened. The building's still there, very modest. You'd think there'd be some monumental construction, considering the magnitude of what happened. There *is* a big new Pyramid downtown, but they play basketball in it.

On my first trip to Memphis in 1990 I saw a quotation from Rufus Thomas on a brass plaque in Handy Park on Beale:

> *My first performance on Beale Street. Here I am at the Palace Theater, standing in the wings. I got butterflies in my stomach. It looks like my life is going to end. And then the emcee says, "Rufus Thomas." The curtain parts. The lights on me. The music hits. My first words come out. And from there on in, the stage belongs to me.*

Mounted on the wall of the bar room in the Blues City Cafe is the left side of a 1958 pink four-door hardtop Cadillac with a long flowing tail fin, in the manner in which, in another place in another part of the world, one might expect a tarpon or a swordfish. There is natural talent here for taking excess and making it natural as sunset. Vegas feels excessive and it's supposed to, but Memphis just feels festive, like an ordinary place with a carnival in town. The motto of the Blues City Cafe is: "If you don't get your food in thirty minutes, thanks for trying." Bonnie Mack is one of the few chefs anywhere who not only has his name on the menu but also has it on the sign out front in fourteen-inch letters. If I had to recommend one restaurant in the United States it would be that one, because the food is great and being there would put you on Beale Street.

A favorite time of the year for some people is the Elvis Festival in August, when the place is inundated with Elvises from around the world. There's the Japanese Elvis, the Korean Elvis, the Mexican who calls himself El Vez and is, they say, pretty good. There is a lesbian Elvis, Elvis Herselvis, who has the ability to cause controversy but puts on a great show and has won over some of her detractors. Not all, but some. A man who enjoys that whole scene told us, "Elvis, y'know, is buried in his back-yard, like a hamster. That's right."

From Tennessee the tour went to the far northwest cor-ner of the country, Seattle, and then all the way back to Massachusetts and then to Washington, D.C. It's a hike from Memphis to Seattle but the weather was good and the roads were dry. For a person who likes the thin-spread parts of the nation, the barren landscapes, the mountains and forests, it was a good time. At Cheyenne you are offered a choice between the northern passage through Billings or the southern through Boise. I took the north-ern line so I could stop in Livingston, Montana, and because it's a little more dramatic and only slightly longer. I–90 climbs Homestake Pass, Lookout Pass, Fourth of July

Pass, goes along the Columbia River Valley and through the Cascades over Snoqualmie Pass.

The long climbs to the passes speak of years of road building and before that the struggles in wagons. Cresting the top the skippers of lead wagons must have looked down those dizzying slopes at the valleys way down there, miles to the floor, and thought 'May God forgive me, but it is one hell of a mess I have brought us into now.' They say many ended up a series of heavy oak splinters strewn down the rocky slope, scattered among a spread of clothes and canvas and the wreckage of trunks; oxen lying broken; wheels gone on ahead by themselves. Years later early semis experienced similar calamities.

Some canyon walls appear nearly vertical, with just enough room on the slope for each pine tree to slide by the one above it, and if you look at it straight-on you see a solid wall of green two thousand feet high. West of the Rockies I traversed the big bleak two hundred miles of unmentioned desert across the eastern half of Washington. Things grow there now and the lacy cool spray of slow-walking irrigation booms surround the traveler. But it didn't feel like farm country, with gnarly brush and sand in the slices between the sprayers, and few farmhouses and no shelterbelts.

For those old-time weathered souls who somehow survived the wooden-wheeled adversities all the way out to

the coast, one would have to guess they were not disap-
pointed. Happy that the endless ocean finally stopped the
wagons and they could settle in and feel all that grandeur
rising behind them, and quit thinking about the other side
of the next range.

Arrival at the ultimate perfect place carries with it the
obligation to live as if one deserves to be there. There is
no better place a little farther down the road, as there is
for all the windblown towns along the way, the places
where people don't feel the pressure to pursue fulfilling
lives of fortune and good taste. The Puget Sound area is
populated mostly by people who were somehow obliged
to settle for nothing less than everything: ocean, mountains, forest, rivers, mild temperatures, lush vegetation,
international cuisine, wine, exotic coffee, the seaport and
everything that goes with it. This may not bring on depres-
sion but it most surely brings on traffic jams.

Took a little walk around the clean and well-ordered
neighborhood of our hotel and marveled at the variety of
plants growing there, everything from magnolias to cacti.
A lot of trimmed bushes. One hedge was trimmed with
each bush rounded on the sides and the top, but flush up
against its neighbor, like buns in a baking pan. The setting
at the gig was also frighteningly beautiful. An outdoor
amphitheater on the grounds of a winery, all too tranquil,
too lush, too fine for a person numbed by twenty-five

hundred miles of pavement in the sustained close proximity of a large diesel engine.

The stagehands were of a general good nature, well balanced, hardworking, no suggestion of gloom anywhere. A peacock with a chest of a fantastic iridescent blue and a gigantic tail that he would spread into a fan too large to fit in a trailer house strolled the grounds around the edges of the action, sometimes displaying and sometimes emitting a piercing and stupidly nasty cry, or a nastily stupid cry. A crudeness comically out of keeping with his fine appearance—and let that be a lesson to us all, not to automatically assume the good lookers have something interesting to say.

We did a fine show to a beautiful crowd and as soon as the trailer doors were closed I headed for the eastbound highway. I didn't mind leaving Seattle, beautiful as it was, because I generally prefer the minor keys and that place is in a major key, cheery and busting with enthusiasm.

Went back the way I came, I–90, and climbed all the same passes from the other side. Stopped at home for one night and kept going the next day, making Pittsfield, in the Berkshire Mountains of western Massachusetts, on Wednesday. It's another beautiful area with a history too interesting to talk about, going back to a hundred years before the Revolutionary War. We were there to do an outdoor show in the Koussevitzky Music Shed, part of the

Tanglewood Music Center and the summer home of the Boston Symphony. The area has also been home to a number of writers, including Herman Melville, Nathaniel Hawthorne, William Cullen Bryant, and, for a time, Sinclair Lewis. An English author with the musical name of George Payne Rainsford James came here in 1851, spent eighteen months, and wrote seven novels in that time.

The Hoosac Tunnel is north a few miles from Tanglewood and is significant for opening a rail line through the Berkshires to the west, the longest tunnel in the USA for fifty years. It's nearly five miles long and cost twenty-one million dollars to finish, ten times the original estimate—an early precursor to the Big Dig, also in Massachusetts—and I mention it because both nitroglycerin and the pneumatic drill were developed for its construction. That jackhammers and nitroglycerin evolved in the proximity of people writing novels and teaching classical music is the sort of thing that just makes me proud to be a citizen of this country.

From there it was an easy drive down to Wolf Trap, America's National Park for the Performing Arts, in Fairfax County, Virginia. Under the copper roof of the marvelous natural wood amphitheater, Ralph Stanley sang "Angel Band" and "Man of Constant Sorrow" and put chills on everybody. It was one of those shows that rang in my ears all the way back to Minnesota.

· · ·

And there it was, the end of another season. We have mixed feelings about that schedule we get every year for the upcoming autumn through spring and into the next July. You look at the last date first, a large outdoor pavilion somewhere, and then backtrack through; check the New York stretch, the long good-weather tour, the couple of shorter winter tours, the home stands. It's a nonoptional menu of your adventures for the entire next cycle. (It does have options but they're like the sign in the home kitchen that says TODAY'S MENU—CHOICE OF TWO—TAKE IT OR LEAVE IT.)

Our time is measured off in these annual increments, the seasons followed by rests, a lot like farming. Different from previous jobs, where the seasons were not so sharply cut and things were allowed to blur together, and you could slide through your life like most people drive the freeway, which is to say without reading the mile markers. Hardly noticing New Year's or your birthday, feeling some guilt through the winter holidays but otherwise fairly oblivious to the passage of the weeks. But with the show there's a punch every week and there's a beginning and an end, and any finish line has a natural pull to it, and when you finally get there you find it less satisfying than you expected. You are another year older and once again wondering how all that could have disappeared so quickly in the truck mirrors.

It was a heck of a season. Revisited some favorite places like Laramie, Memphis, and especially Washington, where I have relatives, some aboveground and others buried in Arlington. Got to spend some time there and appreciate some of the marvels. When archaeologists dig up the ancient wonders of the Mayans and the Greeks, they are digging in that era's Washington. Fans of New York don't like to hear this—all the more reason to say it, I guess—but Washington is the place that really feels like America. The other stunning places out there are all a part of it, but in D.C. you feel like you have seen the essence of what we are about. In spite of all the politicians who you felt didn't deserve to set foot on any part of it, in spite of all the rancor and inefficiency and the wasting of your own money on trying to run your life for you, just walking the mall, with tacky food tents on one end and the Lincoln Memorial at the other, you feel like *This is what we are.* The good and the bad, the misguided and the oddly dressed, all mixed together.

I cruised the museums and saw again the giant stone buildings and walked myself footsore and said Next time I'll have to spend more time here, there's always more than I expect. There is a feeling of tolerance that permeates the place; it's written in stone above your head, everywhere, and it's at sidewalk level. I toured the White House and the Capitol Building and they let me and all the rest of the riffraff just walk in and gawk, right there in the same rooms where state banquets are held and Senate decisions are handed down. I saw the Tomb of the Unknowns and the awed silence of a mismatched crowd, young and old, sitting on the great curved steps, watching a solitary guard march a solitary post amid thousands of bone-white tombstones lined over the green hills of Arlington. We could hear his every footstep.

And of course I spent time at the most American of all contemporary places, the Vietnam Wall: the flowers, the photos set beneath the names, the messages, the families with a piece of paper making a rubbing, seeing the letters come through the page. You see a veteran looking for a comrade and you turn away, overwhelmed, and it's not even about the number, it's about the names and it's about the closeness of it, and the country's awful callousness at the time. A most shameful episode, how we treated our guys back from 'Nam. The angled black stone slices the sidehill like a bayonet. You cannot ignore the wound.

We headed back Sunday afternoon, rose and fell with the soft carpeted mountains of the Blue Ridge and Allegheny, the truck and I, over high canyons on the Pennsylvania Turnpike and then through the foothills on the other side in the tip of West Virginia at Wheeling, and drove deep into the night, passing signs advertising 50,000 HUB CAPS, and EIGHTH WONDER OF THE WORLD FIREWORKS, and TOM RAPER RVS, until the darkness began to lift and we dropped out of morning traffic into a strange truck stop with potholes in the parking lot big enough to fish in and I ordered the Terminator T-Bone and she said "Well done? Medium well?" and by then I was grumpy and said I want it rare, really rare, and if you bring it well done it's goin' back. And it came just right and I wolfed it down and went out to sleep in the truck without even brushing my teeth.

Drove the southern route, I–70, to avoid the cop-infested Ohio tollway and the blithering tollbooth insanity of Chicago traffic, straight west through Indianapolis, took a right in Illinois at Bloomington-Normal and headed north on I–39. Where it joins I–90 there is a pair of unmanned toll buckets and just over the fence on the left a giant water slide, taller than a church. Right there in the tollgate, about ten cars in front, a pickup truck pulling a boat trailer suddenly went dead in its tracks. It caused confusion up there, somehow disabling both stop and go lights, and the traffic sat unmoving in the afternoon heat and humidity while truckers cursed the damn fools over the CB. Other truckers saw the bright side of things: a lot of young women in bikinis standing in line at the water slide. An animated, if politically incorrect, discussion followed. The girls were lucky not to hear it. Finally they began to do the obvious thing up there, channeling into the left lane and just blowing through, even though the sign said something to the effect that video cameras were in use and there was a five hundred dollar fine. I rolled up there and tossed my five dimes in the chute and the light stayed red, same as it did for the guy ahead of me who threw in nothing. And from then on it was easy sailing, all through Wisconsin. A gorgeous day.

I rolled wide open through a backlit forest, the shadows from the tree-lined wide median dappling the left lane, easing side by side real tight past a Peterbilt out of Bourbonnais, Illinois, the driver in dark sunglasses and a large mustache. The lanes were narrowed by orange pylons and I set the trailer wheels just on the bright yellow left shoulder line, traffic ahead and behind, and I slowly gained and with hardly four inches' clearance between our mirrors it occurred to me that I may never get tired of anything this much fun and he looked over and grinned as I began to pull away.

ABOUT THE AUTHOR

RUSS RINGSAK WAS A REGISTERED architect in Minnesota when he bought an over-the-road semi tractor in 1977, a career move that ultimately led him to hauling the equipment and writing for the *A Prairie Home Companion* radio show. He has now been with the show for twenty years—and about half a million miles. He lives in Stillwater, Minnesota, and is also the author of *Minnesota Curiosities.*